The Cadillac Northstar V-8

Also by Anthony Young

New York Café Society: The Elite Meet to See and Be Seen, 1920s–1940s (McFarland, 2015)

The Cadillac Northstar V-8

A History

ANTHONY YOUNG

McFarland & Company, Inc., Publishers
Jefferson, North Carolina

Chapter 1 is adapted from the author's book *The Heart of the Beast*, published by *Automobile Quarterly* in 2005.

LIBRARY OF CONGRESS CATALOGUING-IN-PUBLICATION DATA

Names: Young, Anthony, 1950– author.
Title: The Cadillac Northstar V-8 : a history / Anthony Young.
Description: Jefferson, North Carolina : McFarland & Company, Inc., 2017. | Includes bibliographical references and index.
Identifiers: LCCN 2016040536 | ISBN 9780786471188 (softcover : acid free paper) ♾
Subjects: LCSH: Cadillac automobile—Motors—History. | General Motors automobiles—Motors—History.
Classification: LCC TL215.C27 Y68 2017 | DDC 629.25/04—dc23
LC record available at https://lccn.loc.gov/2016040536

BRITISH LIBRARY CATALOGUING DATA ARE AVAILABLE

ISBN (print) 978-0-7864-7118-8
ISBN (ebook) 978-1-4766-2463-1

Front cover: Rendering of a Northstar V-8 engine; 1999 Cadillac Seville STS (GM Media)

Printed in the United States of America

McFarland & Company, Inc., Publishers
Box 611, Jefferson, North Carolina 28640
www.mcfarlandpub.com

Table of Contents

Preface

The Cadillac 32-valve dual overhead cam (DOHC) Northstar V-8 ranks as one of the most significant V-8 automotive engines of the 20th century. For a unique period of time, it was the only engine powering the entire Cadillac line of cars except the Fleetwood. It also helped to set the technological direction for General Motors in the design of its V-6 engines.

I chose to write a history of the Northstar V-8, the Cadillacs and other GM vehicles it powered because of my familiarity with the Chevrolet LT5 32-valve DOHC V-8 that powered the ZR-1 Corvette. The only thing the two engines had in common was the choice of the valvetrain configuration. I felt the Northstar V-8 was every bit as groundbreaking in terms of sophisticated automotive engine design as the LT5.

When I started the Cadillac Northstar book, I decided to take a different approach to gathering research than I have used with past automotive titles. While interviews with Cadillac engineers would have been beneficial, it was not mandatory, and over the years corporations have grown less open and accessible to researchers and historians. Fortunately, I found practically all the information I needed in published Society of Automotive Engineers (SAE) papers, books, relevant articles, road tests, blog postings and other sources. All images in this book are from GM Media for use in any publication and are cited as such.

Introduction

Cadillac Before Northstar

Among the earliest car companies founded in America was Cadillac in 1902 in Detroit, Michigan. Henry Martyn Leland merged his automotive parts manufacturing business, Leland and Faulconer, with the moribund Detroit Automobile Company. Leland was assisted by his son Wilfred and a team of highly qualified and dedicated men. Lemuel Bowen became president, with Leland Sr., on the board of directors. The new company was named for the French explorer of the land that would one day become Detroit; his name was Antoine de la Mothe Cadillac. Even with its unremarkable body design and single-cylinder engine, the company distinguished itself as a manufacturer with the emphasis on precision and quality. Only three examples of the first Cadillac were built in 1902; these were essentially development cars, and one of these was displayed at the New York Automobile Show in January 1903. Full production was initiated in that year.

Advertising hyperbole was present from the earliest days of the automobile, and Cadillac was no exception. In one of its first advertisements, the new company boasted: "Has 5 h.p. motor, in which is incorporated the best thought, the best effort and the finest construction of the master builders of gasoline motors in this country. Wise agents who are in the habit of 'picking winners' will pick the CADILLAC as the Winner of 1903. Good looking, better acting, and by long odds the best proposition yet offered." The new Cadillac had a list price of $750.

Leland was very much a hands-on engineering manager and was directly involved in the design approval or disapproval of all components to go into the Cadillac, at least initially. Design reviews were held in Leland's office, where he worked to imbue his designers and engineers with his philosophy of precision and commonality of parts. "We must sweat blood for a superior product," he would admonish. "We must make every piston so exact, and every cylinder so exact, that every piston will fit perfectly into every cylinder. This wrist pin must be made accurate to the half-thousandth of an inch. Its bearings must be made with the same precision. Then there will be a perfect fit, and practically no wear-out to it. Otherwise the slightest 'play' means early wear and destruction."[1]

Henry M. Leland founded the Cadillac Motor Car Company in 1902. The first and only model had a single-cylinder engine. Full production commenced in 1903. Leland was committed to an automobile built with precision and quality (GM Media).

It was this attention to precision and quality from the earliest days at Cadillac that established the car company's reputation in the nascent American automotive industry. A four-cylinder model with 30 horsepower was introduced in 1905. The single-cylinder and four-cylinder models continued for more than a decade. Proving the effects of Henry Leland's insistence on precision, Cadillac won the 1908 Dewar Trophy, presented annually for outstanding industry achievements, when three Cadillac Model K production cars were driven, then fully disassembled, their parts mixed into a single heap (and some exchanged with replacements from dealer stock), then reassembled and driven 500 miles, demonstrating true interchangeability of parts.

In 1909, the Lelands and Cadillac board of directors agreed to the purchase of Cadillac by General Motors Corporation. William Crapo "Billy" Durant had founded GM in 1908 after first purchasing and reorganizing Buick and then Oldsmobile. Durant wanted Cadillac for its sound management and reputation for fine engineering. After successful negotiations for the purchase of Cadillac, the Lelands met with Durant in Detroit. The Lelands insisted on a hands-off policy at Cadillac and the

Cadillac's first factory was built on Amsterdam Avenue in Detroit, Michigan (GM Media).

freedom to continue to run the company as they had from the beginning. Durant assured the Lelands that is exactly what he wanted. However, there were troubling days ahead for Durant and for General Motors.

By 1910, General Motors was carrying a severe debt load as a result of Durant's purchase of numerous other companies apart from the brands Buick and Cadillac. In September 1910, a committee of bankers led by James J. Storrow of Lee Higginson and Company in Boston and Albert Strauss of J. and W. Seligman and Company in New York came to Durant at General Motors with the express purpose of either liquidating the two-year-old company or pursuing a refinancing option that put the bankers holding the debt in a more secure position. The senior Leland was overseas on business, and Wilfred himself met with the bankers and pled his case for Cadillac, and by extension, General Motors. Leland first laid out the reasons for Cadillac's market success as a result of its uncompromising engineering and sound corporate management. By the end of the day, he had convinced the bankers not to liquidate Cadillac, because there were numerous companies within GM that had less than profitable units that would be sold.

The bankers had their own ideas of how the running of General Motors could be vastly improved. Through a voting trust, the banks took over operation of General Motors. A loan of $15 million was issued to GM, but under tough terms. This included the demand that Durant step down from the management of the corporation, although he remained a vice-president and on the board of directors.[2] Storrow became interim president of the company for several months, and then Thomas Neal became president.

The New Cadillac V-8

Cadillac engineers then began working on something much larger and more sophisticated. This engine would not be a straight six-cylinder engine as some believed at the time. Instead, Cadillac chose development of an L-head V-8 engine. A number of car companies had proven their capability to design and manufacture a V-8 engine. Rolls-Royce produced a V-8 in 1905, Marmon of Indianapolis displayed its V-8 at the New York auto show in 1906, and in 1908 the Hewitt Automobile Company offered a V-8 in its limousine. De Dion of France introduced a V-8 in its cars between 1909 and 1910. Wilfred Leland began giving serious thought to a V-8 for Cadillac around 1912.

Before laying pencil to paper, Cadillac engineers Charles Kettering and Edward Deeds purchased a V-8 De Dion and in methodical fashion set about studying its design by running tests of it on the engine stand and then disassembling it and examining each part carefully. The engineers also examined a Hall-Scott aircraft engine having a V-8 configuration. The Cadillac V-8 engine program was initiated under the tightest security. The Lelands purchased a building on the corner of Pelham and Drydock Avenues, far from the Cadillac plant, to perform design and development of the engine. When the first development engine was built, it was tested in Toledo, Ohio, and in a Cadillac modified to accept the engine. It performed extremely well and the Lelands approved it for production. Production drawings were released in the summer of 1913. D.

1914 Cadillac V8

Cadillac's first V-8 engine was introduced in 1914. It had a displacement of 314 cubic inches and had a rating of 70 horsepower (GM Media).

McCall White became chief engineer of Cadillac in 1914. White was a graduate of Royal Technical College in Glasgow, Scotland, and went on to work at Daimler and Napier. He had particular experience in high-speed engines and applied this to the V-8's areas of engine breathing and lubrication, as well as other contributions. The final design that emerged was a 90-degree V-8 with a bore of 3.125 inches, a 5.125-inch stroke, displacement of 314 cubic inches and a rating of 70 brake horsepower at 2400 rpm. Cadillac engineers presented a paper before the Society of Automotive Engineers on the new Cadillac V-8 in 1915.

The Cadillac V-8 was introduced in September 1914 in the Type 51 for the 1915 model year. The engine was available across ten standard body styles that ranged in price from $1,975 to $3,600. The Cadillac V-8 was a revelation to the automotive press of the day. One publication, *The Automobile*, drove one example and extolled the car's impressive virtues: "The engineers have provided an eight-cylinder motor of superlative smoothness. The coachbuilders have provided a dignified and luxurious environment. The liquid smoothness of these cars is supplemented by a sense of complete seclusion: the seclusion by a sense of ease and elegance...."[3]

Cadillac had produced a mechanical tour de force that put other luxury carmakers on notice on both sides of the Atlantic. In America, Packard took due notice of this new offering from Cadillac but was not alarmed. The company was secretly at work on its own new engine that would surpass the Cadillac V-8 in a number of ways. That engine was the Packard Twin Six, a V-12 engine introduced in 1916. However, while the Packard Twin Six operated even more smoothly than the Cadillac V-8, more than a few prospective buyers viewed the Packard as perhaps too complex and opted for the Cadillac. Packard offered the Twin Six through 1923, after which it offered a straight-eight cylinder engine and succeeded in topping Cadillac in sales. Before that happened, however, the First World War changed the plans of all automakers for a period and had a profound impact on Cadillac.

Almost overlooked at the time while the V-8 was under development was a Cadillac innovation that would revolutionize the automotive industry. In 1912 Cadillac introduced the electric starter, developed by Charles F. Kettering and an associate, E.A. Deeds, in Ohio in 1909. After receiving a contract from the Lelands to supply 8000 ignition starter sets, Kettering and Deeds formed a company with the name DELCO, for Dayton Engineering Laboratories Co. Extensive testing of prototype units on Cadillac engines revealed numerous weaknesses, and it was several years before the electric starter was proved to be utterly reliable and up to Cadillac standards. It was offered as standard equipment on all Cadillacs for 1912. The innovation was an advertiser's dream, and Cadillac advertised it extensively. It was offered eventually in Buick and Oldsmobile automobiles, and the electric starter was ultimately adopted industry-wide.

World War I and the Lelands Leave Cadillac

In 1914, war broke out in Europe, but it did not have an immediate effect on the United States, certainly not to the degree World War II would. Automobile production continued unabated and there was no conversion to produce war materiel as the United States had not yet been drawn into the war. However, Cadillac would prove a dramatic force in supplying vehicles to armed forces that fought against Germany. Cadillacs both armored and nonarmored were ordered and shipped to Europe.

William Durant had not been idle, and by 1916 had succeeded in regaining control of General Motors. After he stepped aside in 1910 in the management of GM, Durant backed Louis Chevrolet in the development of a light automobile. In 1911, the two men formed Chevrolet Motor Company, and within four years, Durant had succeeded in building Chevrolet into an affordable brand with dealers all over the United States. This new division became so financially successful, Durant used shrewd stock purchases and exchanges with GM stock to regain control of GM and his management of it. The bankers overseeing GM relinquished control of the company to Durant.

The U.S. government was looking to Detroit manufacturers to design and build a new aircraft engine needed for the war effort. The senior Leland wanted to build the engine for the government under contract, but Durant refused Leland's request. Durant was a pacifist and did not want General Motors involved in the manufacture of war materiel. A bitter dispute arose between Henry Leland and Durant over the manufacture of what was to become the Liberty engine. Leland failed to convince Durant of the national need to build the engine and of the benefit it would mean to Cadillac. Leland conferred with his son and other members of Cadillac upper management, and Leland made a momentous—indeed, shocking—decision. The Lelands announced their resignation from Cadillac, as did several other members of management.

Why would the Lelands leave the company they founded, and a car company that in a little over a decade had achieved a reputation as one of the finest cars built in America and the world? Noted Cadillac historian Maurice D. Hendry has little to say about this matter other than the Lelands' disagreement with Durant over the Liberty engine. Surely the Lelands knew the manufacture of the Liberty engine would be temporary anyway, lasting no more than several years, and this involved a product that they had no experience in manufacturing at all. The Lelands were synonymous with Cadillac, so it is a mystery why they would be willing to walk away from it all. There must have been other compelling but unrecorded reasons why the Lelands left Cadillac to enter the nebulous realm of aircraft engine manufacture for war purposes. The executives who left Cadillac with the Lelands included Frank Johnson, Walter Phipps, and Ernest Sweet.

Durant had serious misgivings over the departure of the Lelands and the upper management men who left with them. In fact, Durant reversed himself some months later and agreed to have Cadillac assist in the design and manufacture of the Liberty engine. He even approached the Lelands to return to Cadillac for this purpose and to assume their original positions within Cadillac. The Lelands refused. They had founded the Lincoln Motor Company and were deeply involved in the design of the Liberty engine. The first Cadillac Liberty production aircraft engines were tested in May 1918. Buick also built the Liberty engine, and General Motors' total production before the end of the war that year was just over 2,500 engines.

Postwar Expansion and Production

Two thousand six hundred Cadillac employees went off to war in Europe and many of them returned to resume their work at the company after the war. Production of cars in 1919 reached almost twenty thousand. As Cadillac had grown over the years, it acquired numerous buildings all over Detroit, and manufacture and production of countless parts were scattered around the city. It was apparent to management that manufacturing efficiency needed to be implemented. A new unified manufacturing plant complex was designed and built on Clark Avenue. Construction went on for years and the final phase was not completed until 1927. The manufacturing and assembly portion of the complex now had a capacity of 30,000 cars per year.

During this period, Cadillac initiated a research and development program for a finely balanced crankshaft within the GM Research Laboratories in Dayton, Ohio, managed by Charles F. Kettering. Typical crankshafts were referred to as "flat cranks," but this new crankshaft was referred to as a "quartered" or two-plane crankshaft and became a patented design having drilled counterweights, with machining and balancing done in one manufacturing phase. This advance was so significant, the chief engineer of Rolls-Royce of America at the time, Maurice Olley, predicted the new Cadillac crankshaft would render obsolete all existing or previous designs. The new V-8 with this crankshaft was announced in September 1923 and was built for 1924 and 1925 with the engine code V-63.

The Fisher Body Company was founded in 1908 in Detroit by Fred and Charles Fisher and their uncle, Albert Fisher, to manufacture automobile bodies. In 1910, the Fishers established the Fisher Closed Body Corporation. Cadillac ordered 150 closed bodies, and these were the first fully enclosed cab-style automobiles offered by any American manufacturer. Fisher Body employed numerous innovations in these closed-body designs. These hand-built bodies included interchangeable body parts made off wooden patterns, and were among the first bodies to use insulation to reduce noise and control temperature. Each body received the identification "Body by Fisher," a tradition that continued for decades. Fisher body also manufactured other body styles including open roadsters, phaetons and touring bodies for other car manufacturers.[4]

One of the Fisher brothers, Lawrence P. Fisher, joined Cadillac, and he would soon have a dramatic impact on the company's design direction. Fisher Body became a prime supplier to General Motors and one of the largest employers in America with several thousand employees and the capacity to produce 350,000 automotive bodies a year. In 1919, GM purchased a 60 percent controlling interest in Fisher Body Corporation through a common stock purchase. After the ouster of Durant as president of GM, Fred Fisher was temporarily appointed to the position. Charles and Lawrence Fisher were appointed to the GM Board of Directors and Lawrence was made president of Cadillac. In 1925, Fisher Body acquired a small but distinguished custom body firm in Pennsylvania known as Fleetwood. That year, Lawrence Fisher was installed as general manager of Cadillac at the age of 37. The following year GM purchased the remaining stock held by the Fishers, and all the Fishers were retained to direct the company they had built into such a success.

Cadillac began the design and development of a new model range to be sold along with the Cadillac. That car was the LaSalle. Fisher held strong views that the styling of Cadillacs could be improved. He viewed several of the custom body designs he had seen in a California firm adjacent to a Cadillac dealership during a visit there. It was then he met the designer of those custom bodies—Harley Earl. Fisher observed how Earl used modeling clay to quickly and easily create and revise the designs he was trying to achieve; Fisher had never seen this done before and was impressed. In addition, Earl was designing the entire exterior of the car to give it a cohesive, aesthetic design. Earl took production Cadillac designs and lengthened the chassis and body to give the car more impressive lines and greater interior room. Fisher invited Earl to Detroit to work at Cadillac in the design of its production cars. Fisher, in particular, was interested in having Earl work on a design for an attractive but lower-priced car to sell in Cadillac dealerships.[5]

Earl went to work for Cadillac as a design consultant in 1926. He immediately went to work with Cadillac body engineers on the design of the LaSalle, which was completed in a short period of time. The car would have a 303 cubic-inch V-8 based off the Cadillac design, and two different wheelbases would accommodate the six body styles Earl had produced. The LaSalle was introduced in March 1927 and was well received by prospective buyers. With the most affordable Cadillac that year, the two-door Brougham, having a list price of $2995, the LaSalle two-door roadster sold for $2485, and the seven-passenger limousine for an affordable $2,875.[6] The LaSalle became an immediate market success for Cadillac, and this had a profound impact on Earl's career.

Alfred P. Sloan was now president of General Motors, and the impressive design and sales success of the LaSalle convinced him Earl's design ability needed to be brought to bear on GM cars in general. In June of 1927, Sloan went before the GM Executive Committee to recommend a special department to study art and color in the use of GM automobiles. Sloan added that this new department would have ten designers plus 40 shop workers and administrative staff, with Earl as the department chief. Sloan suggested this new department be called the Art and Color Section. Earl would direct general body design efforts for the car divisions as well as develop color selections and vehicle interior design. The Executive Committee approved Sloan's recommendation. The Art and Color Section would be a part of GM but would operate under the umbrella of Fisher Body. Sloan met with Earl personally and offered him his full support in this new design effort, as this would take from the various divisions design responsibility for the car bodies and interiors.

Cadillac and Packard were the prime competitors in the domestic luxury car market, and each company vied for customers by extolling its engineering, styling and performance. A pivotal year for both companies was 1929. Combined Cadillac and LaSalle sales had continued to climb, from 34,811 in 1927 to 41,172 in 1928. However, sales dropped in 1929 to 35,226 as a significant number of prospective Cadillac owners were lured away to Packard, which had sales of 44,634 cars that year. That year Cadillac introduced its new synchromesh transmission that all but eliminated the accepted gear grinding that often took place during both manual upshifts and downshifts. This was a significant vehicle improvement, and it was an advertising bonanza Cadillac used in boosting its sales. It was such an engineering breakthrough, the concept spread to other General Motors automobiles and to the automobile industry at large.

The Multi-Cylinder Era—Cadillac's V-16s and V-12s with Styling to Match

Even as the LaSalle was being introduced and displayed in Cadillac showrooms, Cadillac had initiated a new engine program to meet the potential needs of a wealthy clientele that would demand greater power and refinement as Cadillac's custom-bodied cars grew longer and heavier. At the same time, research was conducted into how to make their engines run even smoother, and discussions took place on increasing the number of cylinders to meet all these requirements. Initially, the consensus was not to design a V-12 but to double the number of cylinders to 16. The goal was not to double existing displacement but to change the bore and stroke of each cylinder to 3.00-inch bore and 4.00-inch stroke to produce a displacement of 452 cubic inches. By comparison, the V-8 displacement in

The 1931 Cadillac Dual Cowl Sport Phaeton epitomized the elegance of the company's multi-cylinder offerings. An emblem on the radiator grille announced whether the engine was a V-16 (GM Media).

1927 was 314.5 cubic inches and was increased to 341 cubic inches the following year. The angle between the cylinder banks was 45 degrees, making the engine narrow.

The chief engineer of the Cadillac V-16 engine program was Owen Nacker, who was recruited by Lawrence Fisher to join Cadillac in 1926. He was responsible for the design of the 45-degree V-8 for the new LaSalle. Cadillac management and the engineering team insisted on absolute secrecy on this engine's development, and many others within Cadillac had no idea of the existence of the V-16 program. Cadillac wanted the maximum impact when the engine was introduced, scheduled for the 1930 model year. No such automotive engine had ever been built, and it would put Cadillac far ahead of the competition and provide prestige to the other models in the Cadillac line.

An additional benefit of going with the V-16 and its displacement was that the engine's torque characteristics were within the performance characteristics of the existing transmission and driveline, so these could be retained. Overhead valves were selected, along with hydraulic valve silencers. A 5.5:1 compression ratio and dual exhaust resulted in a peak horsepower of between 160 and 175, with 300 foot-pounds of torque. Development engines displayed uncanny smoothness from idle up through the entire rev range. Prototype cars were built and V-16 engines installed, with most of the vehicle development done at the GM Proving Grounds.

The V-16 was meant to power Cadillac's top-tier automobiles, and Fleetwood was brought in to design the bodies that would grace the immensely strong and capable chassis. These body designs were done by Ernest Schebera at Fleetwood, working in cooperation with Harley Earl. The body designs for the V-16 ranged from two-door roadsters to dual-cowl phaetons and 7-passenger limousines, all sharing the same 144-inch wheelbase chassis. In total, there were more than 50 different body styles available in the entire Cadillac line, including the V-16 models. The V-16 models displayed additional chrome-plated steel and polished brass, the most distinctive being the available chrome-plated vents on the sides of the hood. There were additional refinements in each interior as well.

The new Cadillac V-16 was announced in radio commercials during the second week of December 1929, and the first showing of the car was held at the Cadillac factory on December 27. Every automotive journalist in Detroit and others around the country were present with dealers and

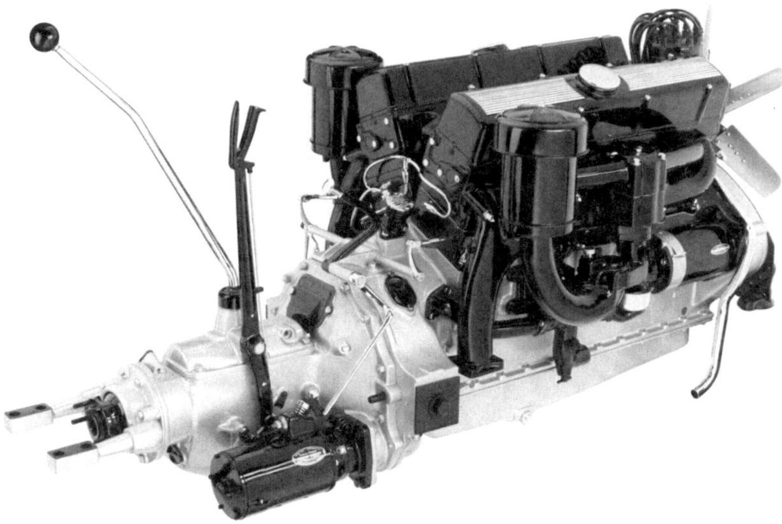

1931 Cadillac V12

The Cadillac V-12 was introduced in 1930 after the introduction of the V-16. The V-12 had a displacement of 368 cubic inches (GM Media).

others invited to see the breathtaking new V-16 Cadillac. These were among the most expensive automobiles in production in America. Prices for the 452-A series ranged from $5800.00 for the four-passenger two-door Coupé to $8750.00 for the seven-passenger four-door Transformable Town Cabriolet.[7] The V-16 Cadillacs were an industry sensation and became objects of desire for wealthy captains of industry, movie stars, and heads of state in Europe and South America.

In September 1930, Cadillac unveiled its 368 cubic-inch V-12 Series 370-A models having 140-inch and 143-inch wheelbases. These models were aimed squarely at Lincoln, Packard and Pierce-Arrow. Prices for the V-12 models were set to be evenly between the prices of the V-8 models and the V-16 models. Thus, the prices made LaSalle and Cadillac models available to buyers looking for a luxury car, practically anything they desired. Among the more notable buyers of Cadillacs were Joan Crawford, Marlene Dietrich, Robert Dollar of the Dollar Steamship Line, Herbert Hoover, Duke Ellington, and Madame Ernestine Schumann-Heink, contralto of the Metropolitan Opera.

1930 Cadillac V16

The Cadillac V-16 was considered the ultimate in refinement and prestige in the luxury car segment during the 1930s. It was a high water mark in Cadillac engineering for years (GM Media).

However, by 1932 the effects of the economic depression America was experiencing were being felt in Cadillac showrooms. Cadillac managed to sell only 296 of its V-16 models. The V-12 models fared better with 1740 sales. Sales of V-8 models came to 2700. Sales were down dramatically for Cadillac and for every luxury brand. Between 1933 and 1934 the entire Cadillac line underwent a significant styling transformation that reflected the hard times the nation was experiencing. Lavish display of wealth—what was left of it, for many—was not socially acceptable, so the design of Cadillacs during this period was decidedly conservative. Despite the sagging sales of its multi-cylinder cars, Cadillac kept them in production because so much corporate prestige was attached to them. These engines and cars were now the hallmark of Cadillac. Additionally, there was a stylistic trend toward streamlining within the automotive industry. A Cadillac advertisement that appeared in 1936 showed dramatically reduced prices on its V-8 models, with the LaSalle listed at $1175, the Cadillac at $1645 and the Cadillac Fleetwood at $2445.

A radically new V-16 was introduced in 1938 that changed the piston configuration from a narrow V to a nearly flat V. The engine was no beauty, but it was decidedly improved in terms of power over the previous engine. The last production year for the V-12 was 1937. The new V-16 was produced for only three years, and Cadillac's multi-cylinder era came to an end. LaSalle's last year of production was 1940. It could be said that 1940 was perhaps the last year that Cadillacs indeed looked like Cadillacs. By 1941 the trend toward more plebeian design was complete. Cadillac had gotten very conservative; it seemed its styling was anything but luxurious and its engineering anything but innovative. It was hard to distinguish a Cadillac from a Chrysler or even a Chevrolet.

During and After World War II

For every American automotive manufacturer, World War II brought passenger car manufacturing to a virtual halt, aside from some production of passenger vehicles built to specific War Department specifications. In February 1942, Cadillac in particular shifted production to the manufacture of the M-5 Light Tank. The drivetrain of the M-5 was pure Cadillac, employing two virtually unchanged Cadillac 346 cubic-inch V-8s coupled to their Hydramatic transmissions with gear ratios required by the slower operation of the tank. Production continued for four years up to the end of the war. Cadillac also manufactured the M-24.

Cadillac passenger car manufacturing did not resume until October 1945 for the 1946 model year. These cars were a continuation of the 1941 models with some trim changes to give them a slightly updated look. Harley Earl would once again play a very large role in the design of postwar Cadillacs. In 1948, the first redesigned Cadillacs in years appeared, with the first modest tailfins that received their inspiration from the Lockheed P-38 Lightning twin-engine fighter of World War II. Engineering innovation had also returned. Cadillac engineer Ed Cole supervised the design of an all-new overhead valve pushrod V-8 designed and built to new levels of refinement and introduced in 1949. Among the most striking of all the Cadillacs of the late 1940s was the fastback two-door Sedanette with its long, sweeping roofline. This car turned heads wherever it went. With the

The postwar Cadillacs first sprouted fins in 1948 and they became a Cadillac styling trademark for decades afterward. The fins on the 1951 Cadillac were subdued compared to those at the end of the decade (GM Media).

new V-8, it was capable of 110 miles per hour. All this Cadillac power, speed, style, luxury and prestige could be had for under $3000.

Harley Earl and his studio designed some of the most memorable Cadillacs of the 1950s; he also designed some of the most innovative as well as memorable Cadillac concept cars that fired the imagination of auto show goers and fueled the sales of Cadillacs. These concept cars were a platform for introducing new design and engineering concepts. Many of these concepts were destined for introduction in production Cadillacs. These showcars included the 1953 Le Mans and Orleans, the 1954 El Camino, and the pillarless four-door Eldorado Brougham displayed at the 1955 Motorama.

All the domestic carmakers were now riding the design craze of fins. With each passing year, fins got larger. Cadillac reached the apex of its fin design in 1959, and even some automotive magazine editors thought Cadillac had gone too far. Some even joked the fins on the 1959 Cadillac were potentially lethal. The chrome trim on the tops was practically knife-sharp, the fins ended in a distinctly sharp point, and even the taillights mounted in the center of the fin's trailing edge also came to a very sharp point. Cadillac listened, and in 1960 its cars displayed more subdued fins.

In truth, the 1960 Cadillacs were probably designed and their tooling ordered before the complaints of the 1959 models reached their peak. In 1959 Cadillac sold 133,733 units. Today, the 1959 Cadillac is viewed as a symbol of excess, while the early 1960s models are viewed with more favor. In fact, fins would remain a design element on Cadillacs well into the 1990s, although not on all models.

Cadillac was unique among the divisions at General Motors and the culture of quality at GM's premier division was pervasive. Just one example of attention to detail involved the "mink test." With respect for the women who rode in Cadillacs who wore mink for evenings out—Cadillac advertising often depicted women wearing mink—Cadillac conducted tests with mink swatches against its leather seating to check for discoloration of the mink or leather, static, or some other undesirable result. Models wearing mink were also taken on tests of up to 50 miles' duration; they got in and out repeatedly during these drives, and both mink and the upholstery (leather or fabric) were checked. It was overheard that the Cadillac test drivers enjoyed this aspect of their jobs the best.

The early 1960s were also the golden age of illustrated Cadillac advertising and catalogs. Automotive illustration was indeed an art, and Cadillac offered some of the most striking examples of automotive advertising featuring this dying art. Difficult to stage or photograph situations lent them-

The 1959 Eldorado convertible marked the apex of fin excess where styling took precedence over engineering (GM Media).

selves particularly well to illustration for Cadillac. By the mid–1960s Cadillac illustration began to fade in favor of simple photography, but occasional examples of illustration continued to appear for some years into the 1970s.

Cadillac began conceptual design engineering and styling on a new front-wheel drive model in 1959. The Oldsmobile division was doing the same thing, and in fact the two divisions would share many of the front-wheel drive components. That year, Cadillac began work on a car to replace the Brougham with what was identified as a new "personal luxury" car. This meant a more individual car with more sporting character, having two doors. This as-yet unnamed car had a very long gestation and development period. After the requisite design proposals and concurrence, the new car program was approved in the fall of 1959. Design and development began quickly with the most tangible evidence taking shape in GM's styling studio as project XP-727. Cadillac had studied the front-wheel drive concept, and Cadillac engineering built a front-wheel drive prototype vehicle that it began testing that winter at a small regional airport in Grayling, Michigan. It was driven in icy and snowy conditions, and FWD proved advantageous in these conditions.

The GM design studio worked on producing a design that could embrace both front-wheel or rear-wheel drive in the event the FWD program was canceled. Several different versions of the XP-700 series were produced at the studio from 1960 to 1962. When Cadillac and GM management approved FWD for this new car, a new styling model, XP-784, was begun. As the design was refined, it progressed into the XP-800 series. With the XP-820 and the design practically finalized in clay form, a fiberglass prototype was built with some other refinements as the XP-825 in the spring of 1964. This design was approved for production and the long-lead tooling was ordered. The drivetrain was engineered by GM Central Research, and the powerplant would indeed be a Cadillac V-8.

In a reverse of GM policy, upper management decided the new production front-wheel drive car to be built by a GM division would be introduced by Oldsmobile in 1966, not Cadillac. This actually allowed Cadillac an extra year of design, development and testing as the assembly line on Clark Street was configured for Cadillac's new personal luxury car, the Eldorado. When the Oldsmobile Toronado for 1966 was introduced to the automotive press, much of the interest and curiosity for FWD was diverted away from Cadillac—at least temporarily. The Eldorado was introduced

For 1967, Cadillac introduced the front-wheel-drive Eldorado on a platform shared with the Oldsmobile Toronado (GM Media).

for 1967, and the car's handsome, unmistakable Cadillac lines were praised by the automotive press. Driving impressions of the car were also positive, for the most part. One road tester took delight in discovering the Eldorado could smoke its front tires under hard acceleration. In short, the Eldorado had more than enough torque and horsepower on tap for any owner's requirements. Introduced in October 1966 for the 1967 model year, Eldorado sold just under 18,000 units in the first year of production.

After the Eldorado, Cadillac models underwent refinement and subtle annual model changes throughout the remainder of the 1960s and early 1970s. In 1967, annual production of all models totaled over 213,000 units. Interestingly, sales of Eldorados continued to increase every year for the remainder of the decade, while sales of the Toronado continued to decline. In 1968 Cadillac introduced its new 472-ci V-8. The displacement increase was not so much to increase power as to offset the increasing demands of the accessory drives and other power demands on the engine. The models in the Cadillac line during his time were the Calais two- and four-door, Coupe and Sedan de Ville, Fleetwood Sixty and Seventy-Five (limousine).

U.S. government intervention in certain aspects of vehicle design and performance started to become evident in the early 1970s with the necessary drop in compression ratios to accommodate lead-free gasoline and in proposed fuel-economy standards and reductions in emissions. Virtually all Cadillac models tipped the scales at over 5000 pounds. Nevertheless, Cadillac sales for 1973 reached 304,839, and in June of that year, the five-millionth Cadillac was produced. Cadillac had been at work on yet another new, smaller model. There was a solid marketing rationale for such a car and that was Mercedes-Benz. In 1973, the Cadillac general manager had toured the U.S. Cadillac dealers and in his discussions with them, the majority stated a smaller, more nimble Cadillac would appeal to a younger and affluent buyer. Many of those buyers were not going for Cadillac but foreign cars like Mercedes and Jaguar.

To make sure Cadillac was on the mark with this potential new car, the luxury division conducted market research in an ambitious clinic involving K-car prototypes in Anaheim, California, in July 1973. Using demographic information, Cadillac contacted 700 luxury car owners to volunteer for an extensive two-and-a-half-hour market research clinic. These people evaluated the Cadillac prototypes against several current competing luxury cars. They drove all the cars, used all interior controls and features, and evaluated the interior appointments. Every spontaneous comment was recorded. The good and bad were duly recorded. Numerous Cadillac executives were on hand for this evaluation. The results of this clinic were applied to the design of the car.

To design and manufacture a completely new model with unibody structure unique to Cadillac would have been prohibitive, so Cadillac surveyed the Fisher Body line and after deliberation settled on the X-car platform used by Chevrolet for its Nova, Oldsmobile for its Omega, Buick for its Apollo and Pontiac for its Ventura. This new Cadillac would share the majority of the glass used in those same models but would have an entirely distinct sheet metal body designed in the GM styling studio. The clay designs that emerged from the studio were quite conservative, having straight lines with nearly flat surfaces. There were definitely no fins. Since this was the first downsized Cadillac in history, the division did not have a smaller displacement engine to power the car. Cadillac had to go to another GM division for its V-8, and the Oldsmobile 350 was selected. However, this 350 V-8 was rated at 180 net horsepower, compared to the 190 horsepower of the bigger V-8 used in the DeVille. With a target weight of approximately 4300 pounds, the smaller Cadillac would have a better power-to-weight ratio.

Cadillac did perform its own extensive suspension design and development for the new car, now named Seville after a long selection process.

Traditional Cadillac ride and handling was important, but this new, younger type of prospective customer also expected sportier handling, and Cadillac engineers worked to satisfy that demand. Cadillac engineered an automatic leveling control system for the Seville. The development cars were extensively tested at GM Milford Proving Grounds and the GM facility at Mesa, Arizona, and in open-road testing in numerous states. Cadillac's Clark Street assembly plant was reconfigured to assemble the Seville. Dealers were accepting hefty down payments for the new Seville in the spring of 1975, even with no brochures yet available at the Cadillac showroom, let alone cars to test drive. Many prospective owners just had a black and white photo from the *Detroit News* to go by, and for them, that was enough. Production of the Seville as a 1976 model (technically a 1975½) began in April of 1975 and deliveries to dealers began shortly thereafter.

Cadillac had provided pre-production models for testing by the automotive press at its Mesa facility in March of 1975. All the top Cadillac executives were there so the press could dun them with questions and the automotive writers could see the "face of Cadillac." In fact, they were allowed to push the Seville wide open during the long stretches as well as take the car through the handling course as fast as their skill would allow. To the journalists' surprise, Cadillac also provided a Mercedes-Benz 450 SE sedan for comparison for them to drive. The Seville received almost universal praise from the editors. Mike Lamm of *Popular Mechanics* wrote: "The Seville doesn't ride, it GLIDES. It's glass smooth, yet the suspension is firm enough so there's hardly any lean in sharp turns. Handling is one this car's very strong points; quick, precise, predictable." Eric Dahlquist of *Motor Trend* emphatically stated, "The new Seville is a smash. Make no mistake about that." And Karl Ludvigsen stated the Seville was "the best Cadillac in twenty-six years."[8] *Road & Track* magazine had never tested a Cadillac but made an exception for the Seville, publishing a complete road test in its October 1975 issue.

The base list price for the fully equipped 1976 Seville was $12,479—higher than any other Cadillac but the Fleetwood limousines—and available options could push it to $15,000. The Cadillac promotion material brazenly compared its new Seville to the Mercedes-Benz 450 SE and even the Rolls-Royce Silver Shadow. The Seville matched the Silver Shadow in cornering power at .67g and in top speed at 115 mph. The Seville was actually quieter at 70 mph than the Silver Shadow, with the Seville reading 66 dB to the Silver Shadow's 70 dB. (These were Cadillac's figures, not those of an independent tester.) First-year production for the Seville totaled

16,355 units.[9] As validation of its competition with Mercedes-Benz, a dealer in Monterey, California, reported four of the German sedans were traded in the first day the Seville went on sale.

There was another milestone resulting from government regulation of the automobile industry that affected every vehicle manufacturer. That was the federal rollover standard that, in its original form, would have effectively wiped out the convertible body style. The legislation was written with regard to roof-crush resistance in the event of a vehicle rollover. Convertibles had no such capability, and with the body style having lost popularity anyway, Cadillac determined its 1976 Eldorado convertible would be the last production year for the car. Other GM divisions ended their convertible production with the 1975 model year. Years later, convertibles did return to the domestic market with changes to the legislation and improvements in what was called "rollover resistance."

Despite the lingering economic recession, Cadillac sold over 309,000 units, a production record, in 1976. The 500 cubic-inch V-8 was replaced in 1977 by a new and smaller 425 cubic-inch V-8 and most of the Cadillac line was redesigned for that year, except the Eldorado and Seville. Vehicle weight was down significantly, with the Sedan DeVille, for example, now weighing 4,220 pounds. Mileage figures were up as a result, but these Cadillacs still had the ride and handling that customers in that market segment wanted. The most striking model was still the Fleetwood Brougham. The Eldorado finally underwent its own complete redesign and the downsized front-wheel drive model appeared for the 1979 model year. Many automotive journalists welcomed the new Eldorado, saying the old one was indeed a behemoth of a bygone era. The new Eldorado was down nearly 1,200 pounds and was shorter by 15 inches. Styling was well received, and the car certainly handled better than before.

Cadillac responded to criticism from some circles that the Seville resembled too much the lines of the Chevrolet Nova, especially in the rear, and that the overall design of the Seville had been too conservative. With the 1980 Seville, all those grumblings were put to rest. Cadillac drew on the classic lines of the Rolls-Royce and Bentley models of the late 1940s and early 1950s in redesigning the rear of the Seville, and then provided much more sweeping lines from the front end to the back of the car with a wonderfully tapered trunk lid. The new car's lines were heightened with the choice of optional two-tone paint schemes. However, the base engine was incongruous for any Cadillac. The standard engine was a 350ci diesel

V-8, which was both noisier and more foul-smelling than the optional gasoline V-8, and had only 105 brake horsepower. Most buyers opted for the gas V-8, and sales of the new Seville confirmed the design was right-on with over 39,000 sold in 1980. Nevertheless, overall sales for Cadillac plunged in 1980 with roughly 239,000 units sold.

In 1981, Cadillac ventured into the somewhat vague "compact luxury" segment, which seemed out of character for GM's premier luxury division. In a rather undisguised venture in badge engineering, Cadillac took the GM J-car platform, exemplified by the Chevrolet Cavalier, with practically all its sheet metal and its four-cylinder engine as well, and produced a Cadillac version called the Cimarron. Cadillac did not want to introduce the car that year because the division had insufficient time to properly engineer the platform so the car would ride and handle as a Cadillac should, and the division also wanted more time to design the sheet metal so the Cadillac identity would be clear. The division was overruled by GM management, and the car was rushed to market in 1981 as a 1982 model. Cadillac tried to distance itself from this car via advertising sleight of hand by announcing the new model as "Cimarron, by Cadillac." Only 13,402 Cimarrons were built in its first year of production. This was no doubt due to the unmistakable resemblance to its Chevrolet sibling. The

The new Seville was introduced in 1980 and its classic car-inspired design was both praised and criticized. The available two-tone paint scheme emphasized the car's lines (GM Media).

Cimarron was not the best bit of automotive marketing in Cadillac history, but most of the buyers of the car had never purchased a Cadillac before, and the division was hoping these new buyers would trade up to larger models later. Nevertheless, government-mandated mileage standards were looming large, and GM wanted as many small cars on the road as possible to help its Corporate Average Fuel Economy (CAFE) standard.

Those new standards drove Cadillac to rethink the rear-drive layout of its largest, most popular models. In 1985, Cadillac introduced redesigned front-wheel drive de Ville and Fleetwood models. Even the Fleetwood 75 Limousine was now downsized and front-wheel drive. As a nod to tradition, however, Cadillac still offered the full-size Fleetwood Brougham sedan. Some prospective Cadillac buyers who saw the writing on the wall ordered their Broughams in anticipation of the future, when such Cadillacs could no longer be purchased. Sales of Cadillacs had rebounded to just over 300,000 units sold in 1985.

A brand-new Cadillac was introduced for 1987. This was the two-seater Allanté convertible hardtop, which had been in design and development since 1982. Responsibility for design of the car's body was given to Pininfarina of Turin, Italy. The initial concept drawings and renderings produced by the famed design and manufacturing firm showed a rakish design which Cadillac toned down considerably. By the time production of the bodies began at Pininfarina, the design was handsome but more conservative. The completed bodies with interiors were air-shipped to Cadillac from Italy and the complete drivetrain with 4.1 liter front-wheel drive V-8 was installed along with remaining equipment. The car featured fully independent suspension. It was by far the most expensive Cadillac in the line with a list price of $54,700. This set the automotive journalism world buzzing and the expectations were high. Weighing 3500 pounds and having just 170 horsepower under the hood, the Allanté was a less than exciting performer. What the car did have going for it was something intangible—exclusivity.

That was something Cadillac sorely needed because the 1987 Seville, Eldorado, DeVille and Fleetwood models shared platforms with Oldsmobile and Buick. Cadillac tried to give these cars some uniqueness with their front end designs. If you lined up the three offerings from Cadillac, Oldsmobile and Buick in ¾ rear view, the cars were virtually indistinguishable. Only the Brougham four-door sedan retained the classic big Cadillac look shared with no other GM division. The Seville had again been redesigned for 1986, having much more pleasing lines than the second generation design but an obvious similarity to the Buick Riviera and Oldsmobile Toronado. Total Cadillac sales for 1987 were down somewhat to 282,562.

There were no dramatic changes in either Cadillac styling or engineering for the remainder of the decade. However, Cadillac had embarked on a significant new "premium engine" design, to use Cadillac parlance. GM's luxury division was about to undergo its most dramatic design and engineering revolution since the glorious multi-cylinder era of the 1930s. This new engine would be unlike any engine Cadillac had ever built. That engine would have four overhead camshafts, eight cylinders and 32 valves. Its name was Northstar.

1

The Chevrolet LT5

Prelude to the Northstar V-8

The Cadillac Northstar DOHC 32-valve V-8 was not the first such engine to be installed in a General Motors automobile. Much of the design, development, durability testing and manufacturing were gleaned from the Chevrolet LT5 engine designed expressly for the ZR-1 Corvette built between 1990 and 1995. The LT5 V-8 elevated the ZR-1 Corvette to the upper ranks of high-performance sports cars in the world with a top speed exceeding that of many Ferraris and Lamborghinis. The LT5 engine program was a costly program for Chevrolet and GM to undertake. While the LT5 was conceived to help the Corvette maintain its high-performance persona, the program was approved with the potential of using this sophisticated V-8 technology at other GM divisions in the future.

The Threat from the Far East

The Chevrolet Corvette remains one of the most iconic automobiles built by General Motors. To American performance enthusiasts it represents the first U.S.-designed and -built sports car, with an eternal popularity. It was also raced professionally in many different classes both in the United States and in Europe. In short, it acquired a well-deserved reputation which Chevrolet protected with a vengeance. It was what one GM executive called a "halo vehicle"—a car that lent great prestige to both Chevrolet and to General Motors. However, in the late 1980s, that reputation came under threat.

During the 1970s, power levels of Corvette engines had dropped dramatically as Chevrolet struggled to meet emissions and mileage standards, reaching a low of 155 horsepower in the base engine in 1975. By 1985, net horsepower was up to 230, but for a Corvette, this was considered barely adequate. Corvette chief engineer David McLellan took this concern to Russ Gee, the director of Chevrolet-Pontiac-GM of Canada (CPC) powertrain engineering. McClellan's office was not far from Gee's, and the two engineers often met to discuss current and future developments that affected the Corvette's performance. This became of particular concern when Chevrolet executives and engineers learned that Honda was developing a new high-performance mid-engine sports car. That car would become the Acura NSX. While Honda made no secret it was developing the car to actually compete with Ferrari, Corvette engineers never saw Ferrari as a threat to the Corvette due to its price level and distinct market. However, this proposed Honda would, indeed, pose a threat to the Corvette, with the NSX having a superior power-to-weight ratio and a significantly lower price than Ferrari.

The NSX could, indeed, pose a significant lure to the prospective Corvette buyer, and Chevrolet knew Honda had the engineering expertise and racing experience to realize a successful super sports car. Honda had commissioned Pininfarina of Italy—with some of the most handsome and enduring automotive designs to its credit—to design the prototype known as the HP-X, for Honda Pininfarina eXperimental. This later was changed to New Sportscar eXperimental, or NSX for short. The design that emerged had a mid-engine 3.0 liter V-6 engine in an all-aluminum monocoque body. In fact, Honda was committed to making as much of the car out of aluminum as possible to improve its ultimate performance and handling. Reception of the concept car convinced Honda to proceed with production.

McLellan and Gee arranged meetings with Bob Burger, general manager of Chevrolet, and with Don Runkle, who was chief engineer of the entire Chevrolet line. Roy Midgley, chief engineer of V-type engines at CPC, was included in these meetings. After examining the known design and performance parameters of the NSX, they were all in agreement this proposed car was a formidable competitor to the Corvette. What could be done about it? To get approval from upper management for a performance project, Runkle arranged an initial meeting with Lloyd Reuss, General Motors corporate vice-president and general manager of CPC. Reuss had joined General Motors in 1957, moved to Chevrolet Engineering in 1959, and worked his way up to chief engineering positions at Chevrolet and Buick over the intervening decades. He was promoted to vice-president and general manager of CPC in 1984. The genesis of the concept of a super Corvette grew out of these meetings.

"I spent a lot of time making sure the Corvette guys were getting resources," Reuss recalled, "and there was work going on at Design Staff and in the Corvette Group to make sure, while we were going through some major changes in organization, that we didn't end up short-changing the Corvette."

The crux of the problem for the Corvette was the state of the engineering art in the small-block V-8 used in the car. The Chevrolet small-block V-8 first appeared in 1955 having 265 cubic inches, two years after the Corvette first appeared powered by the Blue Flame straight six-cylinder engine. The new V-8 naturally found its way into the Corvette engine compartment. The small-block engine grew in displacement to 283, 327 and eventually 350 cubic inches. The late 1960s and early 1970s were the unbridled years of high-performance engine development in the Corvette, carefully watched over by Corvette chief engineer Zora Arkus-Duntov. The apex of small-block V-8 performance was the mechanical lifter LT-1 engine with Holley carburetor having 11:1 compression ratio rated at 370 horsepower. One could go with the 454 cubic-inch big block V-8 that year but with an increase of 20 horsepower and having a considerable weight penalty. After 1970, compression ratio and horsepower began to decline. Net horsepower (rear-wheel) ratings were adopted and a catalytic converter with a single exhaust system appeared in 1975. The late 1970s were not the

GM executive Lloyd Reuss believed the Corvette could be threatened by upcoming high-performance cars from Japan, and championed the super Corvette program that eventually became known as the Corvette ZR1, powered by the DOHC 32-valve LT5 engine (GM Media).

best years for the Corvette, but America's only true sports car soldiered on. Chevrolet investigated turbocharging the small-block for the Corvette, but there were issues of durability and other factors that ruled this out. David McLellan succeeded Arkus-Duntov as Corvette chief engineer in 1975, and his view was that turbocharging was not cutting-edge technology and there would be fuel economy issues. In 1985, Tuned Port Injection was introduced that offered a subtle increase in the engine's power, now rated at 230 horsepower. That, however, would not be sufficient against the much lower-weight NSX.

Enter the British

Another option Chevrolet engineers explored was a V-8 with a multi-valve overhead cam valvetrain. In the early 1970s, Chevrolet had collaborated with the British racing firm Cosworth in the design and development of a Dual Overhead Cam (DOHC) four-valve-per-cylinder head for the 2.0 liter four-cylinder engine in the limited production Cosworth Vega. This car was introduced in 1975 and was rated at 110 horsepower at 5,600 rpm. The base Vega engine was rated at 78 horsepower. Cosworth Vegas developed considerably more power, but certifying the engine for mandated emissions and the addition of a catalytic converter lowered the engine's output. The Cosworth Vega was also sold in 1976, but production then ceased. Chevrolet had a DOHC four-cylinder under development in 1984 but had no experience with larger displacement multi-valve V-6 or V-8 engines. Most of CPC's engine development resources were fully occupied.

"We already had on our plate all these multiport fuel-injection engines," Gee recalled, "so I needed to get some design help."

In November 1984, Lotus Engineering legend Tony Rudd paid Gee a visit in Warren, Michigan. Rudd had one of the finest reputations in the industry in the design, engineering and manufacturing of engines, first at BRM (British Racing Motors) and then at Lotus, where he served as powertrain manager, and later as group engineering director of Lotus. The timing of the meeting was fortuitous. Rudd described Lotus's new DOHC 4.0 liter V-8 used in the Etna show car making the circuits. Gee became interested in this news. Gee did not reveal all that was on his mind, but Rudd was perceptive and sensed Gee might need help in development of multi-valve engines. Rudd mentioned Lotus's multi-valve DOHC manufacturing capability and this hit a nerve with Gee.

"That spurred my thinking onto a V-8 using their cylinder heads," Gee stated. "This was a concept we thought we could develop, putting their four-valve head on our 350 cubic-inch short block. Tony didn't discourage me, but he also said I needed to get over there [to Lotus] ... to see what this would involve because the Lotus four-liter had unique cooling and lubrication systems that were essential to the engine, and we couldn't get that by using the standard Chevrolet short block."

Gee called in Midgley and described the concept of putting a Lotus cylinder head on the Chevrolet short block. As a preliminary effort, Midgley enlarged the proven Cosworth cylinder head design until the cylinder head combustion chamber centers matched the 4.40-inch cylinder bores of the Chevrolet engine block. Then, other requirements followed from that. In the meantime, Gee planned a trip to England to evaluate Lotus, Ilmor, Cosworth, Porsche and a few other companies with respect to this type of program.

When Gee returned to Michigan from his trip, he had decided that Lotus was the best equipped in terms of manpower, manufacturing capabilities and other factors. Over the next several months, numerous meetings took place between Lotus and CPC, both in Michigan and in England, to hammer out the details of what needed to be accomplished—if in fact putting a Lotus four-valve cylinder head on the Chevrolet engine block was feasible. As Rudd and his team of engineers at Lotus worked with the often conflicting requirements mandated by Midgley and his engineers at CPC, they came to realize what CPC wanted to achieve might not be feasible. It began to appear that in order to achieve all the goals both Lotus and CPC wanted to achieve, the engine would have to go with a new cylinder block. The idea of using the Chevrolet cylinder block would have to be scrapped. An all-new cylinder block for the four-valve-per-cylinder head would add dramatically to the cost of the engine. Nevertheless, this was the approach Lotus wanted to take, and Rudd used all his persuasive powers to convince Gee and Midgley of this approach.

"We told them if we made a new block," Rudd stated, "we would be sure of the 400 horsepower because we could have our bore, our stroke and our proportions, and it would be a much lighter engine because it would be an aluminum block ... and much more compact."

The LT5 Is Born

As group vice president of CPC, Reuss held monthly meetings with the body group, the powertrain group, and the chassis/electrical group. In the April 1985 meeting, Gee informed Reuss of the discussions they had had with Rudd at Lotus, and he explained to Reuss the inescapable fact that to develop an engine capable of the power they were seeking—400 horsepower—as well as to achieve mandated fuel efficiency, pass emissions testing, and permit bottom loading of this engine in the Corvette, an entirely new engine would be required. That gave Reuss pause. Such a program would involve millions of dollars that would encompass design, development testing, all-new tooling, manufacturing lines—the list was daunting. GM was going through a restructuring and money was not plentiful. A real cost-benefit ratio had to be established. Such an engine could not be justified on the basis of the Corvette alone; the cutting-edge technology that emerged from such an engine would help General Motors achieve what Midgley called "a balance of values" to improve V-6 and V-8 performance in all areas. And that was how Reuss knew he would have to pitch it to upper management holding the purse strings.

Reuss remarked:

> Throughout a company the size of GM, the financial community does not support projects like this because there is low volume, a lot of expense and high risk. That's not the kind of thing most financial people want to go into. They don't understand the marketing aspect of it and how important some of these things are. There were factions in the company that thought we shouldn't do it, saying, "Why are we spending the money on that?" That was not unique to this program, because as we were going through those years, things got rougher and there was less capital available, almost all the programs would be reviewed. It was an on-going battle right up until we started building engines.

However, Reuss was a veteran at championing various unique automotive programs, and he knew what to present to convince the corporate financial group that it would be a wise decision to finance such an engine program in terms of what the technology could eventually do for other divisions of General Motors. Roger Smith, chairman and CEO of General Motors, threw his weight behind the program because he understood what it meant for the corporation. Together, they succeeded in getting the program fully funded. This would be the first all-new V-8 engine offered in a Chevrolet in decades. Such engine programs typically took five to six years to bring to market. Reuss wanted to cut that in half in order to prevent the program from being canceled before getting to the production line. When Midgley and Gee learned this from Reuss, it was their turn to sit back and think, but they understood the reasoning. Lotus was used to working much faster than GM on an engine program, and that was an asset.

At the news that the new engine program was going forward, McLellan was elated. His task was to make sure the Corvette was up to the output of the proposed engine. There was the matter of the transmission, for example. A new, much more powerful engine would require stronger transmission and driveline components. This new transmission also would need to be designed, tested and built. McLellan had kept Jim Minneker, Corvette powertrain systems manager, up to date on the engine talks that had taken place, and now Minneker was assigned to handle these duties for the new, more powerful Corvette. A new Corvette was starting to emerge, and program insiders adopted a nickname for it: King of the Hill.

When Rudd was informed the new engine program had gotten the GM corporate green light, he was pleased, but was faced with a dilemma. He suddenly had to staff up his various groups. Ian Doble, who had joined Lotus in 1979, was made project manager, assisted closely by David Whitehead as design engineer. Much design work in the mid–1980s was still done on the drafting board, and Whitehead found drawing everything in 1:1 scale very beneficial, as opposed to doing computer modeling, also known then as Computer Aided Design, or CAD. That would come to play a very important part, but old reliable drafting pencil on vellum was still a valid design tool in getting design ideas literally onto paper. Program milestones were mapped out, and they were daunting.

"We really had to pour on the coal then," Rudd remembered, "because by the time we got going it was August 1985 and the plans said the first engine was going to run in May of '86!"

Rudd was also a veteran of numerous engine programs and had been prepared for program approval. To meet the deadlines, Rudd had to triple his engineering staff, and few engineers worked a simple eight-hour day. Ten to twelve hours or more were typical. Much progress had already been achieved based on the experience on the Lotus 4.0 liter V-8. One key difference was Rudd had managed to get Midgley to agree to chain-drive cam sprockets instead of belt-driven cam sprockets. Instead of carburetors, the new engine would feature fuel injection and a large upper intake plenum with individual tube runners going to each intake valve port. Electronic engine controls were crucial to power generation, smooth operation and emissions. To meet the power bandwidth of this engine, two fuel injectors were needed for each cylinder, and that added to the challenge of engine controls.

The challenge for Lotus was to design the engine as compactly as possible to permit bottom loading of the engine in the chassis on the Corvette assembly line in Bowling Green, Kentucky. This was the way the Corvette had always been assembled, with the body being lowered onto the rolling chassis as it traveled down the assembly line. David Whitehead and the other engineers had a challenge of making the engine as small as possible while still meeting the fuel and airflow requirements that would result in the target of 375 to 400 horsepower. For example, the demand by Midgley for hydraulic valve lifters instead of solid, mechanical valve lifters required a wider cylinder head and valve cover.

Considerable design development of the LT5 took place at CPC. For example, all the belt-driven accessory drives and related components on the front of the engine were designed at CPC. The design engineer for this aspect of the LT5 was Gib Hufstader, a veteran engineer who had worked on powertrain design and development there since the early 1950s. He worked with Zora Arkus-Duntov on the packaging of the accessory drives on the Corvette high-performance engines during the 1960s and 1970s. For the LT5, Hufstader selected the location of the starter motor to be between the cylinder heads instead of the traditional location toward the bottom of the engine. Doing this allowed him a tighter packaging of the exhaust manifold and close-coupled catalytic converters.

LT5 Engine Specifications and Development Parts Procurement

At this point in the program, the basic dimensions and specifications of the LT5 were fixed. It was a 90-degree V-8 with a bore and stroke of 3.90 × 3.66 inches with 4.400-inch bore spacing. The cylinder block was cast aluminum with forged aluminum cylinder liners with Nikasil plating. The lower crank case was also cast aluminum having nodular iron crankshaft bearings. The crankshaft was forged steel, as were the connecting rods. The pistons, with 11.0:1 compression ratio, were cast aluminum. The oil pan, which would undergo several redesigns during development, was also cast aluminum. The cast aluminum four-valves-per-cylinder heads were perhaps the most intricate casting of the engine. Intake valve diameter measured 1.540 inches and exhaust valve diameter was 1.39 inches. The chain-driven dual overhead camshafts were cast iron with 0.39 inches lift for intake and exhaust. Camshaft covers were cast aluminum. The aluminum intake plenum was cast in two pieces. The lower portion of the plenum featured two fuel injector ports per cylinder and each bank of cylinders had a dedicated fuel rail. The upper portions of the plenum had a large central induction cavity with individual runners that mated with those in the lower plenum. A single throttle body controlled the amount of fresh air into the engine. The electronic ignition system would undergo a number of refinements during its development. The exhaust manifolds would be individual stainless steel tubes into a collector that bolted up to a catalytic converter on each side.

By November 1985, patterns were being made for the cylinder block, cylinder heads, cam covers, lower crankcase and oil sump. Other parts were being drawn up. The cast iron crankshaft drawing and camshaft drawings were complete. The induction plenum and injector housing were still being designed, as were the exhaust manifolds. Numerous other parts were either being designed, procured, or awaiting design, while other related parts were being finalized. The engine was given the alphanumeric designation LT5. A wood mockup of the engine was completed and sent to Hawtel-Whiting to act as a reference needed for engine clearances inside the Corvette engine bay.

In this time before the widespread use of email, the fax machine was the primary means of conveying design information or questions between CPC and Lotus, which occurred on nearly a daily basis. One engineer stated the program lived or died by the fax machine. Signed approvals were mandatory; verbal agreements were not contractually binding, but were viewed as gentlemen's agreements. The work pace at CPC and Lotus was relentless. Parts from various British and American and European vendors began arriving at Lotus in the early months of 1986. All parts were checked against the drawings and occasionally parts were rejected for being out of tolerance, but that did not happen often. Engine assembly began in April 1986, and it took master mechanics three weeks to ensure everything was absolutely correct. Cam timing was absolutely critical and its verification was closely checked. When it became clear the all-important distributor was not going to arrive on time, Lotus engineers modified an existing unit and designed the hardware to make it perform the same duties for the first engine test.

First Engine Start and Development Program

Roy Midgley had given the target date of engine start for May 1, 1986—the date the entire Lotus team had worked toward. They succeeded. With the engine test room packed with engineers, the first LT5 was started at 2:30 A.M. on May 1. This first test was to check for any oil or coolant leaks and to verify certain performance parameters up to a mere 3000 rpm. The engine test ran uneventfully for 30 minutes and then was shut down. The engine room erupted in cheers. Tony Rudd was in Detroit, and Ian Doble called him with the good news. Rudd gave the good news to Midgley over dinner. This was an impressive milestone in the engine program. Lloyd Reuss was informed soon thereafter.

However, as is often the case with new engine development, Lotus did not have long to celebrate, as subsequent tests revealed numerous unforeseen problems. Chief among them was crankcase oil pressure pushing oil out the breathers above 4000 rpm, and other oil lubrication problems. After some 20 continuous hours of running, the cam chains broke and the reason for chain fatigue had to be determined. The fuel-air mixture was not getting uniformly to each cylinder, and much more study would be needed of the plenum design and injector calibration, as well as refinement of the engine control software. These were among the most critical design development problems.

To resolve the LT5's penchant for pushing its oil out through the breathers, crankcase pressure had to be lowered and a better means of containing oil in the lower crankcase had to be developed. Baffles were added to the interior of the cast aluminum oil pan and a windage tray added so the crankshaft would not whip up the oil above 4000 rpm. Other changes were made internally to improve breathing within the oil passages of the engine. To prevent the camshaft chains from breaking, the initial decision was made to move to a stronger simplex (single row) having thicker links, but these chains also failed during development testing. The remaining option was to change the design from a simplex design to a duplex design, and employ two chain sprockets for each camshaft. These chains survived the 200- and later the 400-hour test cycles. To resolve the problem of unequal amounts of fuel-air ratio entering each cylinder, careful design development had to be done on each of the 16 induction tubes and the design of the main induction plenum itself. There was also a change from a single fuel injector per cylinder to two injectors per cylinder; this offered better performance throughout the LT5's entire rev range, and this in turn improved the task of calibrating the software that controlled engine performance.

Over the next two years followed Phase II and Phase III of the engine's development, which further refined and improved on crucial aspects of the LT5's durability, power, emissions and reliability. At the same time, these engines were being installed in Corvettes for vehicle testing in all sorts of environments. These included hot weather testing in a number of western American desert locations and cold weather testing in Sweden, among other locales. The British engineers were often amazed at the grueling development tests GM demanded of the vehicles, but this had always been the General Motors way.

Engine aesthetics were a key aspect of the LT5's design from the earliest days of the program, as with practically every element of the Corvette. Dave McLellan wanted the engine to be a handsome design and say "performance" from every angle. This had been true of the V-12 designs from Ferrari and Lamborghini, and it had to be true of this engine as well. The LT5 had to convey it was a DOHC design, so the cam covers were designed to convey this unmistakably. To emphasize the message that the engine had four valves per cylinder, eight individual intake ports were modeled on both sides of the engine—one for each intake valve. The top of the induction plenum would have the description "4 CAM 32 VALVE" to remove all doubt. Efforts were also made to minimize or eliminate extraneous emissions-control plumbing that would detract from the appearance of the engine. The engine would be primarily silver in color with either painted components or unpainted aluminum castings, with all accessory drives painted black. The other color added to the engine was that of the red spark plug wires that came from the electronic ignition module at the back of and below the induction plenum with the wires routed between the two camshaft forms of the cam covers. The final LT5 design was a triumph of automotive engine industrial design.

Who Should Build the LT5?

Discussions of manufacturing the LT5 took place early in the engine program. Midgley saw Lotus as the co-developer of the LT5 but not as the manufacturer. Midgley had entered the LT5 program originally thinking Lotus would design it and one of General Motors' engine plants would build it. When he approached the manager of GM engine manufacturing, Dick Donnelly, he was informed the production run would be too small and was not core business, so Midgley should look to an outside engine manufacturer. Midgley came up with a short list of potential manufacturers, most of them in England and America. He booked trips to Lotus and Coventry Climax, and in the U.S., John Deere, Mercury Marine and an underutilized G.M. diesel engine plant in Ohio. Midgley had drawn up a matrix of manufacturing requirements and the decision was self-evident.

"When all was said and done," Midgley recalled, "there was no competition equal to Mercury's extraordinary capability in highly engineered aluminum casting and computer controlled flexible machining."

In the mid–1980s, Mercury Marine was a division of Brunswick Corporation and headquartered in Wisconsin. The MerCruiser division of Mercury Marine was located in Stillwater, Oklahoma. It was here the LT5 would be manufactured. MerCruiser had the engineering talent and manufacturing capability and it had a good grip on supply chain management. It had a vast network of vendors and suppliers already in place that could manufacture and supply many of the required parts for the LT5. The MerCruiser management team, and then the engineering teams, had to be convinced to manufacture the LT5. Midgley successfully won over Joe Anthony, MerCruiser's vice-president of manufacturing, and then Anthony prepared a presentation for the LT5 to the company's management. Once the decision was made by MerCruiser to build the engine, events accelerated. In March of 1986—two months before the prototype engine start at Lotus—MerCruiser received the letter of agreement from CPC stating the company had been selected to manufacture the LT5. It is significant to state here that this was the first time that a division of General Motors outsourced the manufacture of a V-8 rather than manufacture the engine itself. In addition, the engine was to go into the most famous car built by GM—the Corvette.

CPC, Lotus Engineering and MerCruiser personnel began an intense working relationship rarely if ever seen up to that time. MerCruiser was

The engine to power the ZR1 was the LT5. Due to its complexity and limited production, the engine was designed and tested by Lotus Engineering in Norwich, England, and was assembled by MerCruiser in Stillwater, Oklahoma. It was rated at 375 horsepower and was capable of giving the ZR1 a top speed of 185 mph (AutoMasters).

responsible for finding the aluminum foundries to cast all the aluminum components of the engine, and several aluminum foundries were selected from around the United States and England. The same applied to cast iron or steel components. Vendors for the plastic components of the engine also had to be found. Few parts were purchased off the shelf; virtually all were newly designed parts for the new 32-valve 5.7 liter dual overhead cam V-8. One has to remember that the engine was still very much under development and design changes were still occurring.

MerCruiser's first choice for casting the engine block, lower crankcase, injector housing and other critical aluminum components was Dennison Foundry in Dennison, Texas. The cylinder heads were to be cast by Birmal Foundry in England, the same supplier of the development cylinder heads sent to Lotus. The original cast iron crankshaft manufactured for the development engines and the final forged steel crankshaft employed in the production engines were both supplied by GKN-Shardlow, also of England. Each individual component manufacturer was carefully selected based on its existing manufacturing capability and its willingness to manufacture hundreds instead of thousands of parts per year. This phase of vendor selection was part of the ongoing creation of development engines and eventual production engines.

Tragedy struck the LT5 program when John Childs, head of Dennison Foundry, was killed in a car accident. This was a relatively small foundry, and the company struggled under its reshuffled management. The company had been struggling financially, being deeply in debt, and it was forced to file for bankruptcy protection. MerCruiser and Chevrolet management became alarmed. Dennison was the primary, in fact sole, supplier of the LT5's major components. A search for a new foundry began. General Motors had vast manufacturing resources across the United States, and several of its foundries were considered to take over the casting of the critical aluminum parts. GM's Central Foundry in Bedford, Indiana, was selected, but the process took many months. During the transition, Dennison continued to supply contracted parts to MerCruiser.

MerCruiser was responsible for machining the raw castings of the prototype aluminum parts, completing their manufacture, and then shipping them to Lotus. Lotus, in turn, went through their own quality checks, and engines were assembled for development testing both in the dynamometer cells and in test vehicles. One of the most demanding early tests involved a Phase II LT5 engine that was put through an automated test cycle that ran the engine at peak power for five minutes, then peak torque for five minutes, in a sawtooth cycle that was scheduled to run for eight days—if the engine held together. After the 200th hour, the LT5 was shut down. There were no anomalies or failures of any kind. This was a key milestone in the LT5's development. After each development test, the engine was torn down and each part minutely inspected for fatigue and wear. Such inspections, using sophisticated electron microscopes and other means, did reveal weaknesses in the lower crankcase, connecting rods and crankshaft, which resulted in their redesign. The crankshaft, for example, made the change from cast iron to forged steel. Another change resulting from testing was the switch from a simplex camshaft timing chain to a duplex timing chain. The engine was delivering the power goal of 375 horsepower at 6000 rpm.

To manufacture the LT5 within its existing vast building in Stillwater, Oklahoma, a segment of the plant was completely vacated and the manufacturing flow was designed, from all the machining stations to the various subassembly stations and then to the final engine assembly line. This began in the summer of 1987, and as the machine tools arrived, they were moved into their allotted location. The production machine tools came from manufacturers in the United States, England, Europe and Japan.

Another critical development program conducted concurrently with the LT5 was a new six-speed manual transmission which was crucial to the engine's achieving fuel economy goals to avoid the U.S. government's gas-guzzler tax. It also had to be able to handle the LT5's horsepower and torque output, operate quietly, and shift with relative ease. GM did not manufacture a six-speed transmission, so it turned to ZF Friedrichshafen AG in Germany to help. This transmission was the first six-speed manual transmission designed and installed in any GM automobile. It too went through a rigorous development program and ultimately proved to be a very reliable design.

As an example of the quality control MerCruiser was committed to, every rotating part, such as the crankshaft, dual mass flywheel and tor-

The skilled men and women of MerCruiser in Stillwater, Oklahoma, manufactured and assembled the LT5 to exacting standards. The engine was so perfectly balanced and smooth at idle, a nickel could be balanced on the top of the intake plenum (AutoMasters).

sional vibration damper, were carefully balanced, and all such components for one engine were kept together and tracked during the entire manufacturing and assembly of the engine. Once assembled, the engine was balanced again, and evidence of the engine's smoothness was evident in the test cell. Each engine went through a pre-programmed test sequence through its entire rev range, before being crated for shipment to Bowling Green. One day, while an LT5 was idling in the test cell, Bud Agner, director of Stillwater operations, marveled at the smoothness of the idling engine. He decided to take a nickel coin from his pocket and balanced it on the top of the intake plenum. The coin sat there, and as the engine was brought up to 3000 rpm, it simply rotated slowly on its edge. Some months later at a press preview, the same demonstration was performed with the engine idling in a production ZR1 outside the Stillwater plant. The automotive press editors were amazed at the nickel balancing on top of the engine as the driver brought the engine revs up. The LT5 legend began to grow.

ZR1 Corvette Development

During the development of the LT5, test vehicles with these engines were built at Lotus in Hethel, England, and tested throughout England, Europe and the United States. Dave McLellan knew the super Corvette would need the suspension, brakes, wheels and tires to match the capabilities of the LT5 engine. Fortunately, the Corvette was being successfully raced in the United States with some horsepower levels from race-prepared small-block V-8s approaching 400 horsepower. This racing resulted in numerous improvements to the Corvette's suspension, brakes and other components. These served as an excellent groundwork for the yet to-be-named super Corvette under development. Automotive secrets are hard to keep, and the automotive press was very eager to know as much as possible about this new Corvette. In the absence of an official name, Don Runkle at Chevrolet coined King of the Hill and McLellan agreed this would be an apropos name while the car was under development.

Standard production Corvettes built in Bowling Green, Kentucky, without the L98 small-block V-8 engines were shipped to Lotus in the summer of 1986. Development LT5 engines were installed and each car went through complete systems checks before they were taken out on Lotus's test track in Hethel. Lotus referred to these as component cars. Depending on the progress of the engine and car, Lotus would build 20 to 25 component cars for Lotus and Chevrolet to test. The first five completed component cars were shipped to Mosport International Raceway in Ontario, Canada, for testing, as the GM test tracks were not configured to test such a car. High-speed acceleration, braking and handling revealed deficiencies in the oil delivery system, and three of the LT5s were nearly destroyed due to oil starvation. The oil pan was not properly baffled to prevent this and underwent several redesigns before it worked perfectly.

Extreme cold start and drivability tests needed to be performed as soon as possible. In December 1986, such tests were scheduled to be conducted in Kiruna, Sweden, north of the Arctic Circle. Two cars were taken by ferry to Götteberg, Sweden, then driven north. The morning after arriving in Kiruna, the temperature was -40 degrees F. The cars started reluctantly, but shuddered as the cold, thick oil slowly warmed up. A means of warming the oil in the oil cooler had to be devised to smooth the temperature transition. Other diagnostic readings were taken and driving tests were performed in these extreme conditions. Numerous hot and cold weather tests were conducted in the United States and Canada.

Mosport was a key development site for the car. With the new, high-performance capabilities of this car, every system had to be up to the task. High-speed handling and acceleration tests revealed this Corvette needed more rubber on the road, especially in the rear. Additional tests by Goodyear Tire and Rubber Company determined they needed to be 1.5 inches wider than current tires on the Corvette. Goodyear did not make a production tire in this width. In addition, this Corvette would be the fastest production car GM had ever built, and with the top speed of over 175 mph, a new Z-rated tire for the front would be needed as well. The size established for the King of the Hill was P275/40ZR17 for the front and P315/40ZR17 for the rear. Goodyear performed lab tests for six months in the development of these tires, and by mid–1986, the first set of preproduction tires were fitted to special rims to test on the car.

Dave McLellan anticipated the Corvette body would have to be widened to accommodate the new rear wheels and tires. McLellan contacted Jerry Palmer, director of Chevrolet's Design Studio III. This design studio had designed the existing Corvette body that had helped it win the 1984 *Motor Trend* Car of the Year Award. In methodical fashion, Palmer's

The Corvette ZR1, introduced for the 1990 model year, was nearly indistinguishable from the standard Corvette from this angle. It was designed with wider rear fenders and rear fascia to accommodate the much wider rear tires (GM Media).

studio looked at various design themes that would accomplish the goal of subtly increasing the Corvette's rear width from the doors back so it did not look like an afterthought but a sensible evolution of the existing design. In addition, to distinguish this Corvette from the standard car, the rear fascia was redesigned to be slightly convex instead of the current concave design, and the taillights were also redesigned.

The newly designed door panels, rear body panels and fascia began arriving at the Corvette's Bowling Green assembly plant in the spring of 1987, and the first of the pilot-build cars were assembled. After careful evaluation, the alphanumeric for this car was selected. The King of the Hill would officially be designated the ZR1. However, during validation testing of these pilot-build cars that would take place on public roads as well as race tracks, the identification badging remained off the car to prevent drawing attention.

Chevrolet called upon the services of high-performance driving trainers Kim Baker and John Powell to do performance testing of the ZR1 pilot cars and train the engineers in the Corvette group to learn to drive this new Corvette to determine its weaknesses and recommend improvements. In particular, Baker performed tests of the cars at several race tracks around the United States. Among these were Riverside Raceway in California, Talladega Super Speedway in Alabama, and Donnybrooke Speedway (later Brainerd International Raceway) in Brainerd, Minnesota. At Talladega, Baker succeeded in driving the pilot cars at 175 miles per hour, which he considered a comfortable cruising speed. This was accomplished without racing spoilers on the front or rear.

At virtually all points of testing, whether it was on the race track on in cross-country drives with several cars traveling in the same group, anomalies in engine performance or the car were encountered and recorded for resolution. The LT5 was continuing to be refined through these development tests, and engine control software was under concurrent development to maximize the apparent conflicting requirements of performance, smoothness, fuel economy and emissions. Tests continued to be performed into 1988, and there was concern the goal of introducing the ZR1 for 1989 would not be reached. In the midst of the final leg of engine and vehicle testing, MerCruiser in Minnesota was getting ready to build the LT5.

Building the LT5 at MerCruiser

From the time MerCruiser agreed to build the LT5 for Chevrolet and signed the contract, the marine engine company set to work studying the manufacturing requirements and various testing stations required. They were responsible for lining up the vendors to cast all the aluminum parts as well as those for the forged steel components—in short, everything necessary to ultimately produce a running production engine. The precision machine tools that would take raw aluminum castings and produce fully machined parts ready for assembly would take two years from the time the order was placed for them to the time they were delivered to the Stillwater plant. Most of these machining stations would come from Europe and Japan.

A number of unique manufacturing methods were adopted at MerCruiser for the LT5. It was company practice with its marine engines that manufactured parts were sent to a separate quality control inspector who checked the parts against the drawing using precision measuring tools. Due to the limited production of the LT5 and the relatively slow pace of manufacturing, each machinist was himself responsible for inspecting each part he manufactured, and had the authority to reject any part that was found to be out of manufacturing tolerances. Another change was the pace in which design changes for manufacturing was implemented. With MerCruiser's marine engines, incorporating changes on production parts often took months and sometimes more than 20 signatures before the change was approved. This would be impossible with the LT5. A rigorous means of change control was implemented to limit the number of changes necessary; the approval process was limited to a few key personnel who signed off on the change within 24 to 48 hours.

The LT5 team at MerCruiser, with the directive from Chevrolet, established that the first LT5 engine built from production tooling would be started in a dedicated test cell no later than Christmas Eve of 1987. Early in the program, manufacturing engineers from MerCruiser visited Lotus in England and took hundreds of photos of the development engines being built. Lotus technicians then supervised the MerCruiser engineers as they built an LT5 themselves. This was a tremendous aid to the engineers from Stillwater in designing their LT5 assembly line and the chronological steps in the assembly of each major component of the engine, and then the final assembly itself.

The pace quickened when machine tools began arriving at MerCruiser in the summer of 1987 and were positioned on the manufacturing floor as soon as they arrived. After the machine was programmed for its specific part, whether it was the upper or lower cylinder block, the cylinder heads, induction manifolds or other aluminum parts, machining began—not to produce production parts, but to first gain the manufacturing experience and perform tolerance checks of each part. Inspections occasionally revealed defective castings, and these were returned to the supplier. There were Lotus liaison engineers working at MerCruiser, and MerCruiser personnel routinely visited Lotus to make sure any changes in design were correctly incorporated. These changes were usually the result of findings from the development engines, either in the test cells or in the component cars undergoing test driving. Many of MerCruiser's finest machinists and assemblers were recruited to work on the LT5 program.

Hardly a week went by that was uneventful. Whenever a problem or issue arose, there was virtually no red tape to interfere with getting it resolved. Everyone was under a deadline, but when problems arose they were corrected quickly and efficiently. The pace was hectic but each member of the LT5 team came to realize they were working on one of the finest automotive engines ever designed and they went about their work with undisguised pride.

Certain key machine tools still had not arrived by mid–December 1987, and lead engineer Terry Stinson made a key decision. Instead of missing the deadline by waiting for production tooling, he chose to have certain parts machined by trusted outside vendors. For example, the cylinder heads required a very precise camshaft bore machining step performed, so they were flown to the manufacturer of the cam bore machine, and the engineers waited there while the cylinder heads were machined. The engineers then flew with the cylinder heads back to Oklahoma and had the valve guides, valve seats and valve train installed by a specialized engine builder. This same over-the-top procedure was done with several other parts as well. With all parts ready for assembly, just days remained before Christmas Eve.

The First MerCruiser-built LT5 Engine Start

On the morning of December 24, 1987, assembly of the first engine began. The engine block, with all rotating and reciprocating parts, was assembled first. The cylinder heads followed, then the upper and lower induction plenum. Mobil 1 synthetic oil was poured into the filler caps—and then proceeded to pour out of the coolant passages prior to the coolant pump's being installed. The technicians were baffled. They removed the cylinder head valve covers and discovered the necessary core plugs that separate the coolant passages from the oiling passages had not been installed. The engine was completely drained, the cylinder heads removed, the necessary drilling and threading performed, the plugs properly installed, and the heads installed again on the cylinder block. The camshaft timing chains were reinstalled and the cylinder head valve covers installed. Oil was added and there was no oil leak. The accessory drives were added to the front of the engine, ignition and wiring, exhaust manifolds and then the smaller remaining parts. At each step of assembly, a checklist made sure the assembly phase was completed properly.

After the oil had been pressure-fed into the engine to prevent a dry-start condition, the engine on its wheeled stand was moved into the test cell and bolted securely in place. The exhaust pipes were hooked up to vent outside, the fuel line, electrical connections, and coolant lines were attached and coolant was added to the engine and its radiator. The engine was ready. In the test cell were Terry Stinson, Chris Allen, Joe Carroll, Scott Skinner and several Lotus engineers. At 7:00 p.m. on December 24, 1987, the engine was started. For the first second, the only sound heard came from the starting motor while the engine was injected with premium fuel, but then all cylinders fired and it quickly reached its idle speed. All the engineers and technicians cheered. After waiting a suitable period watching the LT5 continue to idle with uncanny smoothness yet making its superb multi-valve, dual-overhead cam sound, Stinson called Bud Agner, manager of plant operations in Stillwater. When Agner answered the phone, Stinson said, "Merry Christmas," and held the phone inside the test cell. Agner congratulated the whole team and then told them to get home to their families.

With the successful start of this first engine, MerCruiser received the approval from CPC to proceed with the necessary steps for production, but there were still development engines to build from MerCruiser's production tooling. Countless changes continued roll into MerCruiser from Lotus and from the field where development cars were undergoing tests. The LT5 was a complex engine and very tightly packaged to permit bottom-loading of the engine on the Corvette assembly line in Bowling Green, Kentucky. With the first Phase IV engine build, MerCruiser discovered the newly designed alternator, which was mounted right underneath the air induction housing of the upper plenum, had an interference fit. The cooling fins on the front of the alternator struck the bottom of the plenum, which meant the engine could not run. Thus, there was yet another change that had to be implemented. There were many more.

Introducing the ZR1 Corvette to the World

Spy photos of a development ZR1 Corvette—taken with a telephoto lens from outside the GM Milford, Michigan, proving grounds—had made their way into the automotive periodicals as early as mid-1987. Initially, Chevrolet planned for introduction of the car in mid-1989 to preempt introduction of the Acura NSX for 1990. Chevrolet made the decision to show the car to the automotive press at the long-lead press preview to be held at Riverside Raceway in June 1988. None of the press was permitted to drive the ZR1 at that time, but later several writers had the opportunity to ride as a passenger with a test engineer at the GM Milford Proving Grounds. All the major consumer automotive magazines, including *Car & Driver, Road & Track* and *Motor Trend,* gave the ZR1 cover stories in their fall issues. Formal introduction of the ZR1 Corvette was planned for the Geneva Auto Show in in March 1989.

In discussions with personnel in Chevrolet Public Relations, Dave McLellan expressed the view it was vitally important where and how the ZR1 could be experienced by members of the automotive press. The ZR1's performance envelope could not be experienced by these editors on the roads of America without running the risk of many speeding tickets.

"We quickly gravitated to the idea that if it was worth introducing right," McLellan recalled, "the only way to do it was to do it in Europe."

With the formal introduction set for the 1989 Geneva show, it made sense for the automotive press to have their chance driving the car at length for the best possible impressions. Rather than giving each of them a car to drive by whatever route they wished, Chevrolet decided to run a caravan of nearly a dozen ZR1 Corvettes from Geneva, through Switzerland and into France along the most scenic route possible—and with long stretches of high-speed highways as well. A preliminary route-finding trip was conducted by McLellan and several others from Chevrolet in January 1989. Hotel accommodations along the route were also important, and this often determined the route ultimately selected. The final destination was the ancient walled city of Carcassonne.

In February, pilot-built ZR1s destined for the European introduction rolled off the Bowling Green assembly line and were driven to Detroit, where they were thoroughly checked out and prepared for the trip to Switzerland. The cars were flown to Marseilles, France, aboard 747s. From Marseilles, the cars were driven to Geneva. The Geneva Auto Show is the premier venue to introduce new models. Despite all the new introductions at the show, the ZR1 Corvette was the sensation of the show. On the day of the drive, a small group of editors were joined by Chevrolet personnel, including Dave McLellan, Jim Minneker and several others who would ride in the passenger seat while the editor drove the car. There were so many editors to accommodate, there would be four separately scheduled trips from Geneva to Carcassonne. Tony Rudd from Lotus was among the privileged first group. It certainly was a time of great joy for Rudd to drive the car that he had worked so hard to bring to fruition, along with hundreds of others at Chevrolet, Lotus, MerCruiser and the countless vendors and contracted personnel and companies as part of the ZR1 Corvette and LT5 programs.

Without exception, the editors marveled at the LT5's immense power, smoothness, and reserves of torque, and the ZR1's responsiveness, handling and braking. The scenic route and the destination made the trip for the editors even more memorable. The editors went back to their respective editorial offices and had nothing but praise for the ZR1. The ZR1 ride-and-drive introduction in Europe was a unique event at the time, but was imitated by other car companies wanting to make a similar impression. It certainly was an expensive undertaking, but totally in keeping with the car. American editors were later finally able to conduct their typical automotive road tests for their magazines and the standard performance stats of 0–60 mph, quarter-mile elapsed time and speed through the timing lights were all the same: 4.6 seconds to 60 mph, covering the quarter-mile in 12.9 seconds going 111 mph. These were just crude numbers that did

Chevrolet chose to introduce the Corvette ZR1 in Europe, where automotive journalists could get behind the wheel and really see what the car was capable of (GM Media).

not begin to describe the capabilities of the ZR1. This was now one of the finest high-performance sports cars in the world—a true threat to the NSX and a warning to Ferrari, Lamborghini and Aston Martin.

In April of 1989, Chevrolet announced it would introduce the ZR1 Corvette as a 1990 model. There were still issues that needed to be ironed out. On July 13, 1989, the first three production LT5 engines were built at MerCruiser in Stillwater, Oklahoma, and after validation testing, were bolted to pallets and shipped by truck to Bowling Green, Kentucky. Chevrolet announced the ZR1 option would add $27,016 to the base list price of the Corvette of $31,979, bringing the total to $58,995. As typically happened with such a high-profile new car introduction, dealers allowed the ZR1s in their possession to sell for far more than the total price listed on the sticker when prospective buyers got into a bidding war. Some eager buyers actually paid over $100,000 for their ZR1. These numbers made news in the automotive press, but the ZR1 would establish even more impressive numbers—numbers that would set world records.

The ZR1 Races into the Record Books

In July 1940, racer Ab Jenkins climbed into his purpose-built Mormon Meteor III, powered by a 1570 cubic-inch V-12 Curtis Conqueror aircraft engine, on the Bonneville Salt Flats. With his illustrious reputation for record-breaking, few doubted Jenkins and his co-driver would succeed. In the next 24 hours, the men broke every world and American Class-A and unlimited record. Some of the records they set stood for 50 years. It was the goal of racer Tommy Morrison to break those records, and he wanted to do it with a stock ZR1 Corvette with a production LT5 engine having 375 horsepower. Many had tried to break Jenkins's records set in the Mormon Meteor III. The most impressive and difficult to break was the 24-hour record with an average speed of 161.18 miles per hour.

Jim Minneker knew from his experience testing the ZR1 that the car was capable of beating this longstanding record. He had accumulated 24 hours of maximum speed on a ZR1, not continuously, but cumulatively. In addition, the LT5 was tested in that demanding durability test between maximum torque and maximum horsepower for both 200 and 400 hours continuously without failure. If any production car could break Jenkins's many records, it was the ZR1, and Minneker convinced Morrison of this.

John Heinricy was the Corvette development manager and an accomplished racer in his own right. He concurred with Minneker, and soon the hope became a plan informally called the Record Run. Morrison agreed he would work to round up sponsors to underwrite the record-breaking attempt, and Heinricy began to look around the United States for someplace where this might best be achieved.

Heinricy looked at the possibility of running the car at one of the NASCAR superspeedways, but the highly banked and relatively short radius turns would put significant loads on both the suspension and the drivers, so these were eliminated. The ideal track would be a high-speed test track with slightly banked turns. Morrison told Heinricy he recalled a conversation he had with racer Bobby Unser, who had raced on the Firestone test track in Fort Stockton, Texas. Unser told Morrison the track was a 7.7-mile oval with slightly banked turns. After sending several people to investigate the track and its facilities, Morrison believed he had found his track.

There was one component on the ZR1 that Minneker, Heinricy and Morrison all agreed would be a weak link: the production tires. During the record attempt, the ZR1 would have an average speed of 175 miles per hour to provide for the inevitable stops, driver changes and possible repairs. The tires were safe at those speeds for brief periods, but not for a sustained period of 24 hours. As the supplier for the Z-rated production tires on the ZR1, Goodyear was contacted to discuss what the tire company might have that could suit the needs of the Record Run. Heinricy and Corvette chassis development engineer Scott Allman sat down with Goodyear's engineers for talks. They learned Goodyear had made a great many different racing tires over the years, but none that would fit the ZR1. Talks turned frank; Goodyear would have to develop such a tire with a clean sheet of paper, and the cost would be prohibitive to the record-setting attempt. After further discussion, Goodyear agreed to underwrite the development of a racing tire for the ZR1 because the company knew the ZR1 and the standard Corvette would be raced. It would be smart business to have this tire in its product line. Design and development testing would take several months, but they would make the tires and have them ready. The Record Run now had the green light.

Morrison succeeded in lining up all the necessary sponsors, including Mobil 1, Electronic Data Systems (EDS) and others. Heinricy, Minneker and Morrison would be among the drivers for the record attempt, and several other experienced drivers were brought in to share driving duties.

Minneker chose a 24-hour development ZR1 as the car to make the attempt, but Morrison and Heinricy wanted a new, stock LT5 installed in the car. They contacted Tim Holland of Lotus working at the Milford Proving Grounds. He said he had two engines in their respective crates that had been recently shipped from MerCruiser. Holland selected the engine and had it trucked to Fort Stockton. Holland was there before it arrived and he supervised its installation in the ZR1. The last week of February 1990 was hectic at the test track in Texas. Practice laps were conducted to thoroughly test the car and get familiar with the track. Testing took place during the day and at night.

Meetings were held to discuss the dangers. The biggest was the potential for coyotes to wander onto the track because the track was not fenced. Hitting such an animal at 180 miles per hour could prove catastrophic. A plan was devised that spotters would be positioned around the track with rifles to shoot or ward off any four-legged interlopers. All the drivers were present and ready. Officials from the United States Auto Club, who would document the speed and times of the car for the Record Run for the FIA, were also present.

On the morning of March 1, 1990, the drivers suited up and had their breakfast. At 9:56 A.M., Heinricy led off first. Each driver's shift was the duration of a tank of fuel, when there was a driver change. Morrison had cautioned the drivers that this was a solitary endurance run, and that they had to concentrate during driving and not become mesmerized. It would be very different from competitive racing, where they could rely on other cars and drivers to keep them alert. Within six hours, five FIA Category A, Group II, Class 10 records fell: the 100 kilometer, 500 kilometer, 1000 kilometer, and 1-hour and 6-hour records. These records were assigned to the L98 Corvette also being raced at the same time with the ZR1. The L98 Corvette came off the test track and the ZR1 motored on.

The ZR1 performed flawlessly hour after hour. As night approached, the first heart-stopper occurred when a coyote wandered into the track, but when it spotted the fast-approaching headlights, it darted back off the track. The drivers raced on through the night. The 12-hour record fell and several others. The sun rose, casting its beams of light across the arid land surrounding the test track. The last driver to get behind the wheel was Morrison. At 9:56 A.M. on March 2, Tommy Morrison broke the 24-hour record held by Ab Jenkins in the Mormon Meteor III for 50 years. The average speed was over 175 miles per hour. Morrison still had one more record to break: the 5000-mile record held by Mercedes-Benz in its mid-engine C111 that had averaged 156.824 miles per hour. The ZR1 had covered 4200 miles at the 24-hour mark, so this final record was several hours away. With eight laps left to beat this record, the car began to overheat and it was brought into the pit area. The hood went up, and a radiator hose was found to be leaking coolant. It was quickly replaced, coolant replenished, and the car was back on the track. The ZR1 broke the 5000-mile record with an average speed of 173.791mph.

This racing and record-setting success further secured the high-performance reputation of the Corvette and fueled sales of the ZR1. It was an advertising boon to Chevrolet and Goodyear as well. The LT5 had indeed proven itself among the finest high-performance production automotive engines ever designed and built.

Crisis in Bowling Green

The precision of every part that went into the LT5 engine, and by extension the ZR1 Corvette, resulted in a car the absolute equal in terms of performance to those cars produced by Aston Martin, Ferrari and Lamborghini. And the NSX had more than met its match. In December 1990, however, the greatest crisis of the car and its engine came to the forefront. MerCruiser received a call from the production manager of the Corvette in Bowling Green that one of the ZR1 Corvettes suffered an engine failure as it was being loaded onto an auto transport. Graham Behan, Lotus liaison engineer at MerCruiser, and Ed Barton, production manager at MerCruiser, flew to Bowling Green to ascertain the problem. They both believed this was an isolated incident and not an inherent design or systemic manufacturing flaw.

Behan discovered that the person responsible for loading the cars onto the transporter had started the engine, immediately revved to over 5000 rpm, and kept it there in an effort to warm up the engine in the cold of December. Behan ordered this be stopped. However, with all the brutal durability testing that had been done on the engine and the car, he could not believe this might be behind the engine failure. Production of the ZR1 at Bowling Green was not stopped, but was slowed. MerCruiser did choose to stop manufacturing the LT5 and implemented a failure analysis of all relevant rotating and reciprocating parts, and an examination of manufacturing quality control of all of the vendors of those parts. All parts manufactured by MerCruiser were within specification.

The problem was narrowed down to one vendor: GM's Bay City, Michigan, manufacturing plant that had machined the camshafts. The plant could not produce the quality control verification documentation. Upon tolerance inspection, it was found the cam journals were not to specification. Bay City immediately tightened its quality control of the LT5 camshafts, and a change to the engine control software was made that limited the engine rpm in cold-start conditions.

Even More Power for the LT5

Engine technology is constantly evolving. The engineers at GM powertrain had been working on improving the performance of the small-block V-8 in the Corvette. They had succeeded in redesigning the engine from top to bottom, and a new generation of the overhead valve pushrod V-8 could now produce 300 horsepower, with more on the way. The LT5 was under threat from within its own ranks. Lotus had been working on further improving the LT5's output and had succeeded in boosting its peak horsepower to 405 horses. Changes had to be made to the engine block and lower crankcase to ensure durability by incorporating four-bolt main crankshaft bearings. Lotus made improvements in the induction ports, incorporating a three-angle valve job to improve air flow, increasing valve overlap, revising camshaft timing and reducing exhaust backpressure. These and other more subtle refinements boosted horsepower to 405 at 5,800 rpm. This engine was approved by CPC for the ZR1 and scheduled for the 1993 model year. In typical fashion, Lotus worked on even further performance enhancements to raise output to between 450 and 475 horsepower. However, the future of the LT5 and ZR1 was already in jeopardy.

In September 1991, Roy Midgley had been informed by his upper management that pending harsh emissions standards scheduled for the mid–1990s would doom the LT5. There was no money to bring the LT5 into compliance with the anticipated high-technology engine controls for such a low-volume engine used in GM's most expensive automobile. That meant the ZR1 itself was doomed. The car had been in production just two years, and all too soon it would have to come to an end. The last production year for the ZR1 was scheduled for 1995. Midgley flew to England

In 1993, Chevrolet announced the last production year for the Corvette ZR1 would be 1995, and engine production would end at MerCruiser in 1993. Engines were prebuilt for the remaining model years, and were prepped and bagged for storage (Anthony Young).

and traveled to Lotus with a heavy heart. Before a packed meeting room, he informed the Lotus engineers and managers that all further LT5 development was to cease. Production of the 405 hp LT5 for 1993, 1994 and 1995 would be limited to fewer than 500 engines per year. Engine production at MerCruiser would actually cease in 1993 with the engines pre-built and shipped to Bowling Green.

The LT5 and ZR1 Aftermarket to Improve the Breed

Numerous Corvette specialty performance tuners had made plans to push the performance envelope of the LT5 far beyond its production capabilities. Most of these aftermarket super-tuners had been involved with improving Corvette performance for years. One of them was Doug Rippie, who performed extensive modifications to eight LT5 engines, resulting in 475 horsepower. These engines received a distinctive black finish and were

The 1995 Corvette ZR1, the last production year, received unique front fender side vents and unique wheels to distinguish the car from the standard Corvette (GM Media).

reinstalled in their original ZR1 Corvettes, which had also received upgrades in suspension and braking components. These cars were identified as the Doug Rippie Black Widows.

The LT5 engine had broken fertile new ground for General Motors, and a new 32-valve DOHC V-8 engine with 4.6 liter displacement was under development to be installed as a premium powerplant in Cadillac's line of automobiles. This new engine offered in Cadillacs would have one of the longest production runs of an engine in Cadillac's history.

2

The Northstar System and V-8

Engineering and Development

In 1988, Cadillac introduced its line of front-wheel-drive (FWD) full-size cars with a new 4.5-liter overhead valve V-8 engine that featured roller lifters and other refinements. It had 155 horsepower at 4000 rpm, and in these cars the power was adequate. The Allanté had an even smaller 4.0-liter (250 cubic-inch) V-8 with 170 horsepower. The largest and only rear-wheel drive model, the Brougham, had a 5.0-liter V-8 (307 cubic inches) with a mere 140 horsepower. All these engines were conventional in their design and engineering, although the roller lifters in the 4.5-liter engine were a technological improvement. The 5.0-liter V-8 had been manufactured for many years. There was nothing inspiring or even exciting with any of these engines, and that was beginning to be a problem for upper management at Cadillac and its engineers.

Nothing stays a complete secret within General Motors among its divisions, and Cadillac had long been aware that Chevrolet had been working with Lotus of England on a new dual overhead cam 32-valve V-8 to install as a high-performance option in the Corvette. In addition, Toyota of Japan was rumored to be developing a new high-end luxury brand to be named Lexus, and Nissan was also developing a competing luxury brand to be called Infiniti. The introduction of both these Japanese luxury brands was for 1989. The cars would be powered by all-new V-8 engines having the latest technology and the highest level of refinement and smoothness at all RPM levels. Mercedes-Benz had a highly developed line of V-8s in cars with an impressive reputation. Ford was also known to be working on a 32-valve V-8 to put in its Lincoln Mark series. Cadillac was staring at competition from all sides and it frankly did not have anything under the hood that could compete, and nothing was planned. In addition,

The Dual Overhead Cam (DOHC) 32-valve Northstar V-8 was the most technically sophisticated engine ever designed by Cadillac. It was the last engine designed by Cadillac engineers before the division adopted GM Powertrain engines (GM Media).

memories were still fresh from the well-intentioned V-8-6-4 introduced in 1981 that was designed to shut down two, then four cylinders from receiving fuel injection in partial throttle or steady-state driving in order to improve fuel economy of the V-8. There were so many complaints about this engine that Cadillac stopped production after one year in its standard passenger cars. The company's image was tarnished over the episode. All of this had to change.

There was a lot of discussion during that timeframe around ideas to power Cadillac with a modern, four-valve-per-cylinder V-8, as this seemed the prevailing trend in new V-8 engine design. Cadillac looked at several architectural alternatives, one of which was to put a four-valve cylinder head—either dual overhead cam or pushrod—on the existing 4.5 liter V-8. This was an attractive concept because it would allow retention of a significant amount of engine tooling. However, Chevrolet had attempted to do this with its small-block V-8 for the high-performance Corvette V-8, but Lotus convinced Chevrolet it was not feasible for a number of interrelated reasons. Chevrolet reluctantly agreed with the Lotus assessment and chose the route of designing a completely new engine. This also became clear to Cadillac.

Within Cadillac, there was the belief that the division should design a new V-8 that would turn the automotive world on its ear, much as the 1949 Cadillac V-8 had done with dramatic marketing effect 40 years before. It became evident that a new engine was needed to bring Cadillac into the 1990s, not to make it competitive, but to strive to surpass the offerings from other luxury car makers. Cadillac initiated an evaluation program of engines then in production, a process known as "benchmarking." The facilities at Cadillac in Detroit soon housed new Mercedes-Benzes and BMWs, but select Ferraris and Lamborghinis were also evaluated because of their dual overhead cams, with four valves per cylinder. This was done to get an accurate picture of the engine state of the art and where Cadillac should really be going.

At the same time, there were engine development programs taking place at General Motors which also had a bearing on discussions within Cadillac. Key among these was the work Chevrolet was doing with Lotus Engineering on Norwich, England, for a multi-valve, dual-overhead camshaft V-8 engine. However, Cadillac was not interested in seeking ultimate power, but what the division called "a balance of values." These included improved engine power-to-weight ratio, effortless power, quietness, and above all smoothness throughout the rpm range.

One of the first issues to be addressed was engine displacement. Cadillac's chief of engineering at the time, Robert Dornan, put forth a series of questions relevant to answering the displacement issue. What does Cadillac need to be to be competitive from a performance standpoint? What is in the Cadillac vehicle portfolio coming up across the line that would use this engine? How big and heavy are these vehicles? How fast do they need to move? What kind of fuel economy was desired with respect to vehicle size and weight? With the right answers to these questions, the engineers could establish how much fuel and air needed to be moved through the engine. It had been established fairly early on the engine would be a V-8 because of Cadillac's history and perception as a big-car manufacturer.

With respect to displacement, once the parameters were formed based on the answers to the above questions, powertrain engineer Sam Weingarden stated the division was looking at an engine displacement of between 4.0 and 5.0 liters. Refining this further narrowed displacement to around 4.5 liters. Then Cadillac went to work on bore centers and came up with 102 mm between the bores and the basic engine block architecture was defined.

During this time, Weingarden's office was three doors down from Bob Dornan's in the same building. The close proximity of Weingarden to Dornan was an essential element for the strategic evolution of this new powerplant for Cadillac. The simple face-to-face contact, often on a daily basis, would facilitate the airing of ideas, talking through design concepts and resolving questions as they came up.

Cadillac management knew it was essential to determine the customer's requirements for this new engine and the cars it would power; Cadillac would not assume it knew what owners wanted in this new engine. The luxury division held clinics and conducted interviews with focus groups made up of prospective customers, many of whom were already Cadillac owners. Out of these interviews a list of desired traits emerged, and based on the number of responses, these traits were ranked in priority. They were:

- Reliability
- Pleasability
- Value
- Precision
- Mass/Inertia/Size
- Engine Efficiency
- Flexibility
- Serviceability
- Technology[1]

Interestingly, nowhere in this list was the requirement for high performance. This may have been due to the Cadillac owner's belief that engine power was always assumed to be adequate in a full-size Cadillac and therefore not listed as a requirement. Put another way, acceleration in a performance car sense was not a requirement to the Cadillac owner. Nevertheless, Cadillac would make sure no owner or magazine editor would find any reason to complain about the Northstar V-8's performance.

Northstar V-8 Structural Components

The 90-degree V aluminum engine block was designed as a two-piece unit with the parting line at the crankshaft centerline. The lower crankcase extended 92 mm from the crankshaft centerline. This allowed for maximum stiffness to the overall engine block and support of the crankshaft throughout its performance range, and facilitated manufacturing and assembly procedures. Four 10-mm bolts were used at each bulkhead to fasten the lower crankcase to the engine block. To the lower crankcase was mounted a unique oil distribution plate with channels designed to line up with grooves and holes in the lower crankcase to direct oil to the pump and the crankshaft. This distribution plate eliminated the need for long, drilled oil passages in the cylinder block. The engine block was an open deck design, unlike the traditional cast iron V-8 engine designs. The open deck design was selected after finite element analysis to determine bore distortion.

This engine would employ iron cylinder liners and an open deck design suited to the design parameters. The diameter and wall thickness of the iron liner were carefully determined to account for installation during manufacture and liner retention during maximum operating temperature. The differing thermal expansion of aluminum engine blocks and iron crankshafts had always been carefully studied since the lightweight material became common in production engines. Cadillac performed detailed studies of the variables that affected manufacturing tolerances in the main bearing area. Cadillac chose to use an aluminum-lead alloy bearing as the optimum solution for the Northstar V-8. As with practically any new engine development program, the Northstar V-8 engine block and lower crankcase proved to be a challenge to bring to production, according to Northstar V-8 program manager Sam Weingarden.

The issue that proved to be the greatest problem was the die-cast aluminum block with the cast-in-place iron liners. This was not common engineering practice at the time. Cadillac did a significant amount of process development, die development and solidification modeling to get the block right and of high quality.

The crankshaft was designed using cast nodular iron, deemed more than adequate at the targeted level of power and anticipated owner driving patterns. The casting process incorporated technological improvements in alloy casting procedure to improve the mechanical properties of the crankshaft. Fillets between the crank journals and counterweights were rolled for better fatigue properties. Like virtually all other components in the Northstar V-8, computer analysis was employed on the crankshaft bearing widths and diameters of the connecting rod and bearing journals.

The counterweights were also designed in this manner. The main journals were cross-drilled for improved lubrication.

The cast aluminum piston was conventional in design, and unique in having four machined relief notches in the top of the piston to provide clearance for the intake and exhaust valves. The piston had a steel top ring, cast iron second ring and a three-piece oil control ring. The forged steel I-section connecting rod had balance pads on both sides at the crankshaft end so grinding could be performed to precisely balance the assembly. The floating piston pin was also conventional in design.

The cylinder heads were Cadillac's first dual overhead cam design for a production V-8. Inlet valve diameter was established at 33 mm and the exhaust valve diameter was 29 mm. Both valves had a stem diameter of 6 mm. The valve diameter and intake and exhaust valve lift were engineered to achieve high flow efficiencies. The combustion chamber was designed to optimize the four-valve configuration to achieve the best flow of fuel and air, attending combustion and exhaust for the lowest emissions and power generation. Studies were performed to achieve low detonation sensitivity and high diluent tolerance. The spark plug was placed 1.5mm from the chamber centerline toward the exhaust side to have consistent intake side fuel position. This bias improved combustion and minimized detonation sensitivity under load.

The one-piece cylinder heads, cast with the semi-permanent mold process using a special 319 aluminum alloy, were unique to the right and left banks of the engine. The intake mounting flange was 45 degrees to the centerline of the engine. The main oil galleries were drilled the entire length of each cylinder head using high-pressure gun drills. Each cylinder head was designed to be assembled with the camshaft cover installation sealing the head, prior to installation on the cylinder block. At that time the camshaft simplex chain assembly was installed. Cadillac employed a two-stage cam chain drive. A camshaft drive sprocket was driven off a chain sprocket powered by the crankshaft. The camshaft chains were driven off this secondary camshaft drive sprocket. The camshaft chain tensioners were hydraulic and had spring-loaded mechanical anti-backlash ratchets to ensure quiet engine starting.

The Northstar V-8 induction system underwent several prototype designs and this actually proved to be the most problematic of the whole engine development program and subsequent production. The first production induction unit was manufactured in magnesium, a material rarely used in engines manufactured by General Motors at the time of the Northstar's introduction. This unit was referred to by Cadillac engineers as "the magnesium bucket." Sam Weingarden recalled the issue with the magnesium intake manifold.

Other problems were discovered during development. When the engine was shut down, and depending on how the valves were parked, there would sometimes be unburned fuel in the intake manifold. Upon starting, this residual air/fuel in the manifold would occasionally backfire. Cadillac had to do ignition development work and go with a separate ignition coil system to get around that issue.

Cadillac had rarely used magnesium for engine components in the past. The division had to learn the metal's peculiarities during manufacture and in production. While extremely light, the manifold did have to be strong enough to survive a major engine event without cracking. The magnesium was used during the engine's first year of production. During this time, GM undertook a new development program to use a composite induction manifold. This program went far more smoothly, and this material was eventually selected for installation on later production engines.

As originally introduced, the induction system comprised the magnesium plenum housing holding glass-filled thermoplastic induction tubes, the nylon fuel-rail assembly with fuel injectors, the manifold air temperature sensor and the manifold absolute pressure sensor. The precision-cast magnesium induction plenum eliminated many of the machining steps that might otherwise be required. The intake throttle body was bolted to the front of the magnesium intake plenum. The positive crankcase ventilation (PVC) system and the exhaust gas recirculation system (EGR) had for decades been vital systems in the reduction of engine emissions. Both PVC and EGR were integrated into the Northstar V-8's design.

With a greater number of rotating and reciprocating parts as well as the cam chain assembly compared to conventional overhead valve designs Cadillac had engineered previously, the lubrication system of the Northstar V-8 was unique to the division's history. A new clamshell-type georotor oil pump was designed and was driven directly off the crankshaft. The oil passages to the main bearings were cast into the lower crankcase. The cam chain tensioner and overhead cams received oil from a groove passage behind the number one main bearing. Careful thought was given to the oil passages for the valvetrain to eliminate any startup noise. The seven-quart oil pan was designed with baffles and a windage tray to minimize oil displacement during high rpm and hard cornering situations. Northstar V-8-powered Cadillacs would have an oil life monitoring system that measured various parameters including coolant temperature, oil temperature, number of revolutions and starts, mileage and time, and would inform the driver when an oil change was necessary.

The Northstar V-8's cooling system was also unique. Due to the cam chain drive and accessory drives at the front of the engine, the coolant pump with its inlet and outlets was mounted at the rear of the engine and driven by the left bank intake camshaft. This was also done to reduce the complexity of the external coolant plumbing. The Northstar V-8 was designed with a safe mode operation so if coolant was lost, the engine control module would alter the engine's cylinder firing from eight to four cylinders using its overheating protection circuit. This operation, coupled with the engine's lubrication system, would prevent engine damage so the driver could get the vehicle to a service facility and not be left stranded. The starter motor was mounted between the cylinder heads, similar to the arrangement on the Chevrolet LT5 installed in the ZR1 Corvette.

The Northstar V-8 ignition system incorporated four ignition coils with related control electronics housed in a single module. Two crankshaft position sensors and one camshaft position sensor relayed this information to the module upon turning the ignition key just prior to starting. There was a special wheel mounted to the crankshaft to ensure fast synchronization during starting. Information from the crankshaft and camshaft sensors permitted precise synchronization with the first 90 degrees of crankshaft rotation at starting. The Powertrain Control Module (PCM) used the signals from these sensors to control spark and fuel injection scheduling and other engine control functions and readings and diagnostics. There was a built-in failsoft function that permitted engine start and run in the event of a sensor failure.

This single PCM controlled and integrated both the engine and the transmission during operation. This ensured seamless operation of the powertrain. At the heart of the PCM was the dual microprocessor having 128k of memory. The PCM handled all aspects of fuel delivery, amount of intake air, spark scheduling, emissions monitoring and other engine control functions for optimum fuel economy, emissions and engine performance. The PCM also controlled transmission shifting based on acceleration and load, even taking into account the traction control system.

With the first-generation Northstar V-8 and its transverse layout, the Allanté and subsequent FWD models were designed with a single exhaust system. The left-hand exhaust bank (at the front of the vehicle) had to pass between the engine and transmission, and over the transmission before joining with the right-hand exhaust bank and into the close-coupled 170-cubic-inch catalytic converter. After the converter, the single exhaust pipe was routed toward the rear of the car and an exhaust muffler/resonator. The entire exhaust system was designed to have minimum restriction while achieving mandated, tighter emissions limits.

Another key fact soon made itself evident during these discussions regarding this FWD engine—a new transmission would be needed. Dornan pulled together the entire Cadillac vehicle team with the powertrain engineers. Dornan established the need for a system, not just an engine. This would eventually evolve into the Northstar System. It would embrace the engine, transmission, suspension and braking systems as an integrated whole. This new engine would have significantly more power and torque than existing FWD engines in the Cadillac line, so using existing transmissions was quickly ruled out. Consequently, there would also be a new generation FWD transmission to mate to the new engine. Separate engineering teams were established for the engine, transmission, suspension and ride control, braking and the overall vehicle.

The Cadillac Northstar V-8 Road Tests

The FWD Northstar Cadillacs were first available in select 1993 models. In its last year of production, the hardtop convertible Allanté featured the 4.6-liter Northstar engine. The automotive media had been somewhat put off by this car's breathtaking list price since its introduction in 1987, and the inclusion of the Northstar V-8 for 1993 did not change the attitude of the auto writers very much. The Allanté was being phased out in favor of the newer Seville and Eldorado with the Northstar, so there were not too many journalists willing to test drive Cadillac's current "halo car."

One auto journalist who did was Jim Mateja of the *Chicago Tribune*. The Allanté had been operating with a rather unremarkable 200 horsepower 4.9-liter V-8. For 1993 it received the 295 horsepower Northstar V-8. However, the newspaper reporter was shocked by the car's price tag of over $62,000 when he looked at the car's window sticker in October 1992.

The Northstar V-8 was first available in the sporty two-seater Allanté in 1993. In terms of power, it was a dramatic improvement over the standard OHV V-8 (GM Media).

Low volume was one reason, as only 2000 Allantés had been sold on average per year since its introduction. Mateja admitted the 1993 car was dramatically better than earlier years in terms of ride, handling and definitely acceleration. The 1993 model could reach 60 mph in seven seconds and had a top speed of 150 mph. The Northstar V-8 transformed the car. He noted the engine was uncommonly quiet and smooth, yet the exhaust note even at idle was pleasant. Where the car failed was fuel economy. The Allanté achieved a rather poor EPA city rating of 14 mph and the car had to be sold with a gas guzzler penalty of over $1500. Mateja, however, was impressed with the car's ride and handling at speed and under all road conditions. The road-sensing independent suspension, speed-sensitive steering and excellent traction control, even in wet weather, made the car safe and enjoyable to drive. These were the benefits of the total Northstar System.

The Cadillac Seville had received a stunning new body design for 1992. In 1993, the 295 horsepower Northstar V-8 was standard in the STS, while the Seville SLS retained the pushrod V-8 for that year. Despite this, the main automotive magazines like *Road & Track* and *Car & Driver* rarely tested Cadillacs; these two publications were very European-focused, unless the American car in question was the Chevrolet Corvette. *Motor Trend* was more domestic-friendly. *Consumer Guide* tested many cars each

The Eldorado underwent a complete redesign for 1992 and became much more sleek in appearance. The Northstar V-8 became available in this model in 1993. Styling of the 10th and last generation Eldorado remained unchanged until its last production year of 2002 (GM Media).

year as part of its overall consumer product focus, and this included Cadillacs.

Many prospective Cadillac buyers did not read the automotive magazines, but for them *Consumer Guide*'s evaluation carried a lot of weight. The magazine's review of test cars was always objective to the point of boredom, but could be relied on to give an honest appraisal of a car's overall performance. The smooth and powerful Northstar V-8 in the Seville STS received high marks for its performance, especially about 3500 rpm, but low marks for its fuel economy. The car's handling was very firm but, over some rough road surfaces, jittery. Overall, the magazine in its review said, "Especially in STS trim, the Seville is Cadillac's best premium sedan in ages...." The editors felt the Seville STS was a worthy opponent to the BMW 740iL, Lexus LS 400 and Infiniti Q45. Cadillac had indeed hit all its design and overall performance objectives against the competing brands and models. The Eldorado Touring Coupe received the Northstar V-8 and ride and handling enhancements in 1993 as well.

In 1994, the full-size Cadillac DeVille Concours received the Northstar V-8 and was the subject of a complete road test by *Motor Trend* magazine. The extended test of this car actually appeared in the August 1995 issue in order to include feedback from Concours owners. The Northstar V-8 installed in this car had a different cam profile for its four overhead camshafts to improve low-end torque while lowering horsepower somewhat. The engine was rated at 270 horsepower and now had 300 pounds-feet of torque. This helped to move the nearly 4000-pound Concours out smartly. With the perfectly programmed 4T80-E electronically controlled four-speed transmission, the editors could achieve 0–60 in 7.8 seconds. One editor test driving the car exclaimed, "This car has serious pull. What a fabulous engine!" Gas mileage was improved and the Concours sold without the gas guzzler tax. The editors managed to achieve an average real-world gas mileage of 17.7 mpg.

Acceleration alone was not the whole Concours story, however. This car was what Cadillac was traditionally known for, but it was also a reflection of the GM division as a true technology leader, as the editors noted. When this new generation of Cadillacs was conceived and designed, they

The Northstar V-8 became part of the Northstar System in Cadillac's full-size sedans in 1994. The Northstar System also included proprietary engineering for the suspension to enhance ride, handling and braking in such models as this Sedan DeVille (GM Media).

The 1994 Concours with Northstar V-8; having slightly more horsepower made this the quintessential Cadillac of the early 1990s (GM Media).

would be entirely new and would embrace the Northstar System. This also meant speed-sensitive steering that was effortless at low speeds and offered less assistance at highway and otherwise brisk driving modes. Likewise, the Road Sensitive Suspension electronically adjusted the dampers depending on the car's speed and cornering. While some of the owners complained the car's ride was on the harsh side, these were probably traditional Cadillac owners not used to the new sporting nature of the Northstar-powered cars. The editors at *Motor Trend* felt the suspension was tuned just right for most drivers. Technology also found its way into the brakes, which featured a Bosch anti-lock braking system that proved its impressive performance on wet roads under hard braking that prevented loss of vehicle control.

Apart from technology, the Concours, with a base list price of \$36,590, exuded all the traits Cadillac was known for. On its nearly 114-inch wheelbase, all six passengers had impressive leg room. The sumptuous leather seats provided comfort for hours of driving, and the vast trunk could hold suitcases for all passengers with room left over. The styling of the DeVille for 1994 was an aesthetic success—handsome from every angle and unmistakably Cadillac. Many of the Concours owners stated their car was the best Cadillac they had ever owned.

In 1996, *Motor Trend* also tested the Seville STS. The editors seemed more impressed with the interior appointments and changes to the '96 model than what the car offered in acceleration, handling and overall performance. They had tested a 1995 model the year before, and that might explain it. The car still had musclecar-like acceleration with a 0–60 mph time of 6.4 seconds and covered the quarter-mile in 14.7 seconds as it churned out 300 horsepower at 6000 rpm. These are impressive numbers for a car with an engine having only 279 cubic inches. Interestingly, the standard H-rated Goodyear Eagle tires that came standard on the STS mandated a top speed imitation of 130 mph. If the optional Z-rated Eagles were ordered, the car was limited to 150 mph. If the speed was indeed

The Cadillac Concours came standard with a higher output Northstar V-8 giving the sedan impressive performance for its size and weight. This is the 1998 Concours (GM Media).

limited to 150, one wonders just how fast the STS was capable of going. Cadillac would not say.

The editors at *Motor Trend* also had the opportunity to test a 1998 Seville that was significantly improved in its ride and handling while displaying subtle body restyling. Cadillac had been at work to make the Seville more competitive with Europe's luxury sedans like Mercedes-Benz and the large BMWs. That was a tall order but the magazine editors felt Cadillac had achieved it with the 1998 Seville STS: "The Seville is easily the most technologically advanced production car GM—perhaps the U.S.—has ever produced, and based on our initial impressions, can be safely called the best sports/luxury sedan built in America. In most areas, we were pleasantly surprised by levels of performance, control, luxury and pampering convenience that, yes, are worthy of its world-class ambitions."[2]

The Northstar V-8 underwent subtle improvements over the next several years, but the cars themselves were the focus of Cadillac's on-going product improvement. The 2000 DeVille DTS tested by *Car & Driver* actually astonished the editors. The first tipoff that things were really changing at Cadillac was the invitation to go the Phoenix International

The Seville was completely redesigned for 1992 and was one of Cadillac's most successful four-door sedans (GM Media).

Raceway to test the 2000 models. Before the editors were given the cars to drive, the Cadillac engineers gave them pointers on braking into the corners and what to expect with the car's handling. The first fifteen minutes behind the wheel earned newfound respect from the editors for the large luxury sedan.

"To our shock and amazement, the most sporting version of this new DeVille, called the DTS—for 'DeVille Touring Sedan'—did more than merely survive this trial by tire. It was astonishingly composed and capable, by any standard."[3]

Editor Csaba Csere aggressively drove the car along the Riverside Raceway track and marveled at the DTS's ability to handle high speed corners under hard braking. The car did not display the behavior of similar luxury sedans of plowing and tires howling. The Cadillac's StabiliTrak system coupled the Continuously Variable Road-Sensing Suspension (CVRSS) and its antilock braking system transformed the DTS into one of the best-handling large sedans made in America. Accelerating out of the corners was very impressive with the 300 hp Northstar in the DTS. Also contributing to the car's handling capability was the very rigid third-

In 2001 the full-size sedan was redesigned, and the DeVille Touring Sedan became the DTS (GM Media).

generation G-body introduced for 2000. The rubber-mounted sub-frames helped to insulate the interior from road noise. The rear independent suspension had a total of ten inches of suspension travel, and with automatic load leveling, the car could comfortably carry six adults. The base list price for the 2000 Cadillac DeVille was around $42,000. The DTS with other available options pushed the price to $47,000.

Cadillac's full-size sedan featured redesigned sheet metal for 2006 to embrace the prevalent Art & Science design theme of the other Cadillac models. The DeVille name was gone and DTS was adopted in keeping with the naming convention of the other models. However, underneath that sheet metal there was little that was new. It still rode on the same FWD G-platform that drove other full-size GM offerings from Buick, Oldsmobile and Pontiac. In fact, the DTS was mechanically identical to the Buick Lucerne, which could also be powered by the Northstar V-8 (see Chapter 7). The DTS was to keep this sheet metal until the end of its production with the 2011 model year, which also marked the end of Northstar V-8 production.

Little attempt was made to make the DTS particularly more sporting; Cadillac had other models in its lineup for that. The DTS was for a particular, older Cadillac owner and the luxury division did not want to alter

The DTS received an all-new body design in 2006 and retained this handsome style until the end of its production run in 2011 (GM Media).

that. Cadillac did offer a 1SE preferred-equipment option that altered the cam profile of the Northstar V-8 to provide roughly a 10 percent boost in horsepower with a subsequent slight reduction in torque. With this option, horsepower rose from 275 to 291 at 5600 rpm with torque at 286 lb.-ft. at 4400 rpm. With a curb weight of 4212 pounds, the DTS reached 60 mph in seven seconds flat, covered the quarter-mile in 15.4 seconds doing 92 mph, and had an electronically limited top speed of 125 mph. The FWD Northstar V-8s did not receive variable valve timing and other performance enhancements of the second-generation Northstar V-8 designed for rear wheel drive applications.

Car & Driver editor Robin Warner wrote in the road test of this car that appeared in the September 2006 issue, "The 1SE also has a different shift algorithm and suspension tuning although it doesn't make the DTS feel like what we would call a performance sedan. But for a car this large and nose heavy (over 60 percent of its weight rests on the front tires), its body motions seem well controlled. Even during a spirited, tire-squealing trip around an interstate on-ramp, the DTS takes a relatively flat set and maintains course."[4]

The DTS was the last Cadillac model powered by a Northstar V-8, with the last production year being 2011. There would be a model year lapse until the DTS replacement reached the market. This car was the V-6-powered XTS. Surprisingly, this V-6 had over 300 horsepower on tap. But for lovers of refined Cadillac V-8 engines powering a four-door sedan with incomparable ride, excellent handling, supreme quiet and marvelous luxury, their love affair ended in 2011.

3

The Next Generation

The Northstar V-8 for Rear Wheel Drive (2004)

At the dawn of the new millennium, Cadillac management began to lay plans for a series of new rear-wheel drive vehicles based on its successful and proven Northstar V-8. Cadillac wanted to offer a new vehicle for an emerging market niche identified as a crossover. Loosely defined, a crossover was an automobile with more of a utilitarian body configuration more akin to a station wagon, but having a higher stance than a car. While Oldsmobile, Pontiac and Chevrolet had always built station wagons, Cadillac never had, and the luxury division wanted to avoid any such connotation with this new vehicle. Cadillac embraced crossover as a new and trendy marketing identifier. At the same time, this vehicle was to also be luxurious because, above all, it was to be a Cadillac.

At roughly the same time, the Evoq concept was in development, and its enthusiastic reception at auto shows in America and Europe gave the push for Cadillac to pursue the development of a production rear-wheel drive (RWD) sports roadster that would become the XLR. In addition, other vehicles planned for the future would also be rear-wheel drive, and this was the motivation for Cadillac to purse a redesigned and improved Northstar V-8 for RWD applications. By this time, all four-cylinder, V-6 and V-8 engines were designed within General Motors' GM Powertrain division.

This new RWD drive application of the Northstar V-8 would also permit higher output in terms of both horsepower and torque, and GM Powertrain would employ new technologies to achieve this. The engine technologies to be examined and employed were four-cam continuously variable valve timing, low restriction intake and exhaust manifolds and cylinder head ports, a stronger steel crankshaft, electronic throttle control, and close-coupled catalytic converters for improved emissions.[1] With this RWD Northstar came the requirement for a new transmission in order to have a true, next-generation powertrain to rival any other luxury V-8-powered vehicle in the world. Cadillac and GM Powertrain also made program goals to reduce levels of noise, vibration and harshness (NVH).

Even more sophisticated math-based 3D computer modeling and analysis and simultaneous engineering were employed with the RWD Northstar V-8, coupled with much existing hardware, reduced development time and required development hardware. With the maximum number of common parts, manufacturing implementation was also realized more quickly. However, this new RWD application was initiated with concurrent design development of an all-wheel drive (AWD) application for the crossover vehicle starting with the 2004 model year. The FWD Northstar V-8 received mid-generation improvements for the 2000 model year. These included new low-friction valvetrain with roller finder followers

Northstar RWD
2004 4.6L V8 (LH2)
for Cadillac XLR

The Northstar V-8 was re-engineered and reconfigured for a whole new class of rear-wheel drive (RWD) Cadillacs for the 2004 model year (GM Media).

which improved fuel economy, a low-restriction center feed inlet manifold to lower induction noise under hard acceleration, and the introduction of air-injection reaction (AIR) for reduced emissions. Among the goals for the RWD application with close-coupled catalysts was the elimination of the AIR system. Variable Valve Timing (VVT) was also new.

General Configuration

The RWD Northstar V-8 retained the same 4.6-liter displacement with 93.0mm bore and 84.0mm stroke. It retained the same 64.4mm crankshaft main journal diameter and the same 54mm crankshaft pin journal diameter. Basically, the RWD block and lower crankcase were identical to that of the 2000 model year engine dimensionally, but there were new parts. The new model employed a new forged steel crankshaft to handle the anticipated naturally aspirated power increase and future

The second generation Northstar V-8 engine upper block designed for RWD was an open-deck design and permitted better engine coolant flow around every cylinder (GM Media).

supercharged applications (see Chapter 4). This permitted manufacturing efficiencies that helped to reduce development costs.

The RWD engine block was a high-pressure die cast aluminum casting made of ASTM B85 SC102A alloy. As before, the iron cylinder liners were cast-in. The liners themselves were centrifugally cast of ASTM A159 G3500 iron alloy. The lower crankcase was squeeze-cast ASTM B85 SC84A aluminum alloy. Four M10 bolts secured the lower crankcase to the block at each bulkhead with precision-located dowel pins ensuring alignment. Virtually all new engine block components were designed using Unigraphics and finite element method performed to determine stress points and optimize coolant flow. The RWD block shared the same open deck and Siamese bores as the FWD block. The new block differed primarily in the manner of coolant routing. In the RWD block, the coolant is routed in and out of the front of the engine, as opposed to the back of the block in the FWD application. GM Powertrain spent considerable time refining the coolant flow in the RWD block using CFD analysis.

The block differed also in the inclusion of cast oil passages up to the cylinder heads for the VVT system; VVT was not added to the FWD Northstar V-8. Additionally, the engine mounting locations differed from those on the FWD engine. The lower crankcase was also unique in the RWD engine in order to accommodate the new transmission being engineered concurrently. The RWD lower crankcase had a variation in the oil distribution plate employed in the FWD engine. M8 bolts for the oil pan were used in place of the M6 bolts on the FWD engine to add rigidity for AWD applications. There were added oil lubrication requirements for this new RWD application due to increased acceleration and handling capability, particularly with respect to the XLR roadster. Lengthy development was required on the XLR because of the tight under-hood environment in that car and the need to have a shallow oil sump and orienting the engine 0.5 degrees forward. A dry sump system was considered for the XLR but was rejected due to operating noise levels. Also, in the SRX crossover, the Northstar V-8 was angled upward 3.5 degrees. The differences for the RWD Northstar used in the XLR and the SRX were with respect to lubrication. These involved the design of the oil pan, oil pickup tube, and oil filter adapter. The oil pans were radically different for the two applications. For the XLR, the front of the oil pan was necessarily shallow to clear the vehicle cradle and this oil pan required an oil level sensor and perforated baffle for the shallow section to minimize windage

Bottom view of the 2004 RWD Northstar V-8 upper block (GM Media).

effect of the crankshaft. For the SRX, the oil pan was deeper with a shallow rear segment to clear the steering rack. In addition, the SRX oil pan had a cast passage for the AWD axle to pass through it.

With the RWD Northstar, the cylinder heads would incorporate the new variable valve timing camshafts. This required new head design as well. The same single-piece water jacket was employed from the FWD head, and this permitted predictable analysis on the coolant flow. Additional slots were added in the cam bearing cap area to increase critical lubrication there. These heads had a higher compression ratio of 10.5:1, made possible by the VVT system, and the combustion chambers differed accordingly. Additional machining was performed around the exhaust valve area in the cylinder head to unshroud the valves and improve exhaust flow into the exhaust manifolds. In addition, the exhaust ports were now oval. The intake and exhaust valves were the same specification as the FWD.

The valve angles and cam bores were identical to the FWD engine, retaining these machining setups. Primary machining steps differed in the front and rear of the head, and the exhaust manifold bolting pattern on the right cylinder head. The new RWD heads retained the flexible graphite with perforated steel core gaskets, with the addition of steel grommets for the high-pressure VVT oil feed holes. These heads did retain the original roller chain cam drive setup as the FWD Northstar V-8. The intake valves were 3mm larger, at 36mm.

Variable valve timing was not a new technological advance, having been in volume production in various engine applications for over 20 years, but was particularly advantageous on the multi-valve RWD Northstar V-8. GM Powertrain determined that both intake and exhaust camshafts should have VVT in order to meet the demanding goals for

The cylinder heads for the RWD Northstar V-8 were a completely new design while retaining the advantageous four valves per cylinder (GM Media).

Variable valve timing (VVT) was introduced in the RWD Northstar V-8s in 2005. This improved engine response under various conditions such as hard acceleration (GM Media).

RWD application. These requirements included: "ease of starting, rapid converter light off, the smoothest possible idle quality, excellent part load torque, fuel economy and maximum wide open throttle performance across the engine speed range."[2] An added bonus of employing VVT was the elimination of both EGR and AIR emission systems employed on the FWD engine.

Variable valve timing is achieved by what is referred to as phasers. There are two basic types to achieve VVT: helical-spline phasers and the vane-type phasers. After evaluating both methods, GMP selected vane-type phasers because of their smaller size and lower mass. The attendant disadvantages of vane-type phasers were outweighed by the inherent advantages. Basically, VVT operates in such a manner that each individual camshaft can advance several degrees or retard several degrees using a cam sensor target wheel, an electromagnet and an integral control valve. The control valve itself and electromagnet were electronically controlled by the Electronic Control Module (ECM), which responded to throttle input requirements. Significant development was directed toward the VVT control valve so that it was quick in response, stable in its operation and durable for the life of the engine. The camshaft covers were also unique to this engine due to the VVT system. The entire cylinder head subassembly with VVT system was fully assembled and could be bolted to the engine block at the Northstar engine plant, after which the chain drive was assembled.

It was decided to employ a new forged steel 1538MV microalloy crankshaft for both the RWD and FWD Northstar V-8s. The main journal and rod diameters were maintained from the previous FWD crankshaft. The rod and main bearings were a bimetallic aluminum-silicon alloy, and measured 4mm with the steel backing. The connecting rods were forged from a ferrous powder metal blank. The aluminum alloy pistons, however, were not forged, but cast from hypereutectic alloy.

The FWD and RWD Northstar V-8s employed the same composite intake manifold. These manifolds were manufactured using the lost core process and made from glass-filled PA 66, a polyamide. A plenum duct was mounted to the front of the intake plenum, and the throttle body was mounted to this plenum duct.

On the exhaust side, the manifolds were made from high silicon/molybdenum nodular iron. The close-coupled catalysts were welded, not bolted, directly to the exhaust manifold with a stainless steel exhaust pipe with flange on the exhaust side of the catalyst to permit bolting of the exhaust system for the RWD application. The designs of these exhaust assemblies for the XLR and the SRX were different. Specifically, the catalysts were moved closer to the engine for added clearance with XLR frame members.

This new RWD Northstar V-8 had an improved engine management system to integrate the VVT and other engine refinements to optimize all aspects of engine performance. While this new ECM exhibited a higher level of complexity in its command and control ability, it resulted in refinement of engine performance from idle to wide-open throttle and steady-state cruising. The ECM and the plethora of sensors within and on the engine and within the vehicle that fed information to it were the most sophisticated to date.

The cooling system for the RWD Northstar V-8 was naturally different from that of the FWD application due to higher output and added loads of the optional AWD feature. The radiator and hose routing was different between the XLR and SRX. Computer analysis modeled the flow of the coolant throughout the engine, coolant pump and the radiator. Specific attention was paid to the coolant flow around areas of the exhaust valves and the coolant passages were optimized using CFD analysis.[3]

Improvements in Northstar V-8 Manufacturing

A full two years prior to production year release of the second-generation Northstar V-8, GM Powertrain initiated extensive quality initiatives in the manufacture and the assembly of the engine at the corporation's Livonia, Michigan, engine plant. This was part of an early launch production program. The first quality initiatives were implemented for the 2003 FWD Northstar V-8 engines, and further initiatives were added for the RWD Northstar V-8. There was a fundamental change in mindset, or culture, and manufacturing methods as part of this initiative. The Livonia plant was the first to adopt GM's Global Manufacturing System (GMS). The plant installed new engine assembly and cylinder head subassembly lines, upgraded machining operations, improved error-proofing using the latest technology equipment, and improved cold-test equipment after final assembly.

Part of the GMS called for proactive involvement of engine assembly personnel in order to improve assembly, inspection and feedback of any assembly issues, no matter how seemingly insignificant. This was meant not only to improve the Northstar V-8s but to also instill ownership of the work by the line operators as part of the quality initiatives. The Livonia engine assembly lines for the existing FWD and forthcoming RWD Northstar engines were reconfigured so both engines could be manufactured side by side. A new two-loop assembly line was created, with one assembling the shortblocks (minus cylinder heads, induction system and accessory drives), and a second loop where assembly of the engine was completed.

New machining equipment was installed having what was called agile machining capability. These new machining stations were capable of producing machined surfaces in microns, or millionths of an inch, and each agile station with its multiple machining heads was capable of machining different areas of the cylinder blocks or cylinder heads as well as different parts while reducing setup time. The agile lines could differentiate between FWD and RWD parts and machine those parts to precise specifications. The FWD and RWD cylinder heads were subassembled on new lines.

New error-proofing steps were incorporated from the part identification, machining, subassembly and assembly phases. Crankshaft bearings, for example, underwent the following steps in error-proofing:

1. First loaded onto a fixture that checked to make sure the right set of bearings for a particular engine have been selected and automatically loads them into the block.
2. Testing of the assembled short block in an automatic "torque-to-turn" test that would spin the crankshaft, check for proper tightness and cleanness, and blow air through the oil passages to check backpressure.
3. Performed another "torque-to-turn" test after installation of the cylinder heads and timing chain.
4. Checked for vibration in an accelerometer as part of a final cold test of the engine.[4]

An extensive series of cold-test procedures were performed on each assembled engine that monitored the cylinder heads, cylinder block and other areas in a functional test without actually passing fuel through it. Once the engines were approved and signed off by the line technician, the engines were shipped to the vehicle assembly plant, and once installed were given a fueled, running test to complete the vehicle assembly prior to shipment.

New Hydra-Matic Five-Speed Transmission

Concurrent with the development of the RWD Northstar V-8, GM Powertrain worked to upgrade its 5L40-E transmission to handle the added torque and power of the engine, and incorporate three new performance-enhancing features into one transmission for the first time. This new five-speed transmission was the 5L50-E.

"The 5L50-E was designed specifically to manage the high torque and horsepower of the next-generation Northstar 4.6 liter DOHC," stated Rich Mardeusz, the assistant chief engineer for this transmission, "while combining the convenience of an automatic transmission with the feel of a high-performance manual transmission. And it does it in the same size package as the 5L40-E."[5]

The three-in-one performance features of the 5L50-E included Driver Shift Control (DSC), Performance Algorithm Liftfoot (PAL) and Performance Algorithm Shifting (PAS). DSC allowed the driver to switch from

Cadillac reengineered the Northstar V-8 to permit rear-wheel drive. It was used to power such vehicles as the newly redesigned 2005 STS sedan (GM Media).

automatic to clutchless five-speed performance manual shifting. Once the shifter was moved into DSC mode, the driver simply tapped the lever to shift upward or downward. The transmission control module, or TCM, protected the engine and transmission in DSC mode by monitoring the vehicle speed, engine torque and load, and the gear currently used. The PAL prevented upshifts during engine braking and could determine engine and vehicle speed and deceleration in order to determine one to two gear downshifts. The PAS helped to match optimum gear selection during high-speed cornering by monitoring engine speed and lateral acceleration.

The all-wheel drive (AWD) option in the SRX was a new fulltime drive arrangement improving its handling, acceleration and braking performance, offering improved traction and vehicle control in wet or wintry conditions. The AWD was also fitting with traction control as a safety enhancement.

Magazine Road Tests of the XLR and SRX

Cadillac had unveiled the XLR roadster at the January 2002 Auto Show. The car on display at the show was not a production vehicle, but visually was identical to the 2004 model that would roll into showrooms in the fall of 2003. *Road & Track* editors were able to test the XLR for the June 2003 issue. *R & T* wanted to remind readers of what Cadillac once stood for: "Big fins and whitewall tires. Vast expanses of gleaming sheet metal and glittering chrome."[6] That had not been the case for many years, but perhaps the editors were nostalgic for the iconic Cadillacs of the 1950s. In describing the XLR, the editors agreed the car was an order of magnitude beyond anyone's perception of what Cadillac had been. That new perception had already been introduced with the re-engineered and redesigned Eldorado and Seville. The XLR was a completely different kind of Cadillac with its aggressive looks and a more powerful front-engine, rear-wheel-drive sporting machine.

R & T editors had always placed a performance priority on 0–60 mph and quarter-mile times, top speed, cornering G's and braking distance. They were pleasantly surprised to experience the XLR reached 60 mph in only 5.6 seconds and covered the quarter-mile in 14.0 seconds doing 102.6 mph through the timing lights. On the skidpad, the XLR cornered at 0.88 G's and it could brake from 80 mph in 217 feet. It had an electronically limited top speed of 155 mph, but with some knowledgeable removal of the limiting circuitry, the naturally aspirated XLR was capable of significantly higher top speed.

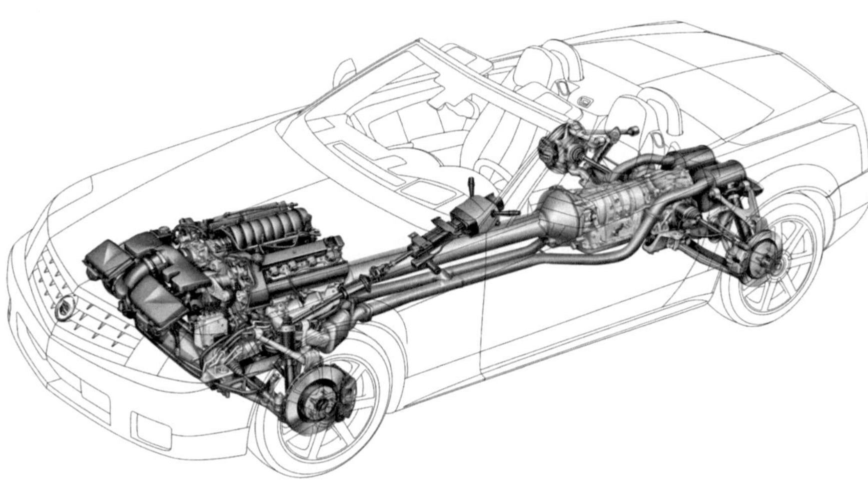

The XLR featured a transaxle design that improved the front-rear weight balance of Cadillac's XLR sports car (GM Media).

The XLR had a unique driveline compared to the SRX. Like the Corvette, the XLR had a five-speed transaxle, and this gave the car a front/rear weight balance of 48/52 percent. The editors gave the XLR high marks for what this transaxle did for overall performance, saying it performed "in an effortless, nearly transparent fashion. Full-throttle upshifts and downshifts feel practically seamless, exhibiting none of the abruptness sometimes associated with higher-horsepower automatic applications."[7]

Perhaps the only unpleasant surprise of the test was seeing the sticker price. List price of the 2004 XLR with no options was $75,435. This was fully $30,000 over and above a 2004 Corvette. The XLR was aimed squarely at the Mercedes-Benz SL500 roadster and Jaguar XK8, among other high-performance European two-seaters.

Car & Driver also published its road test of the XLR in June of 2003. After discussing all the features of the car readers would want to know, editor Csaba Csere stated what the performance of the XLR was like: "The Northstar V-8 fires immediately and settles into a smooth idle every bit as refined as the XLR's competitors deliver. The engine maintains its upper-crust demeanor as you slip it into drive and accelerate up to a cruising pace. When the revs climb beyond 5000 with your foot to the floor, the Northstar produces a lovely patrician growl that lets you know it's working hard but still not breaking a sweat."[8]

Editor Csere also like the XLR's handling capabilities and was suitably impressed with the car as it navigated twisty roads. He credited the confidence-inspiring driving to the car's extremely rigid chassis structure, its superbly engineered suspension with its magnetic ride control, and its Michelin MXM4 P235/50R-18 tires. In the end, the tough-to-please editor had to agree the XLR was a worthy contender to the Mercedes-Benz, Jaguar and Lexus competitors. The XLR was manufactured in the Bowling Green assembly plant, which was the home of the Corvette.

The SRX, on the other hand, was manufactured in GM's Lansing Grand River Assembly Plant in Lansing, Michigan, where the V-6–powered CTS was manufactured. Magazine road tests of the SRX did not appear until September 2003. *Car & Driver* tested the Northstar V-8–optioned SRX that month. Almost immediately, the editors pointed out the steep price tag for the Northstar-equipped SRX; with just a few options it listed at $48,520. With the AWD option and mandatory options that came with it, the total came to over $59,000. The editors stated this put the AWD SRX in the same market segment with the Porsche Cayenne S,

Infiniti FX45 and BMW X5. The boxy SRX was designed to be a serious people and cargo hauler, having 32 cubic feet of cargo space.

The same 320-hp Northstar V-8 was available in the SRX that was standard in the XLR. The editors marveled how quiet and smooth the engine was at idle. "Drop the hammer, and the SRX lunges with rapid shifts from the GM Hydra-Matic five-speed automatic and fruity snorts from the twin tailpipes," the road test stated. "The variable cam timing plumps up the V-8's low-end grunt and throttle response so there's power stuffed in every corner of the SRX's tach. Traffic-light tears and on-ramp launches are effortless."[9]

While the sport wagon handled well enough over twisting smooth pavement, the editors reported the SRX shuddered and clomped over bad pavement, while transmitting some of the suspension response to the steering wheel and seats. They used the BMW X5 as the high water mark of isolating such jarring feedback from the driver. However, the editors also agreed handling over such rough pavement could be resolved, checking off the optional $7,145 Luxury Performance Package with AWD and sophisticated magnetic ride suspension.

The test closed with comments from three of the editors who drove

The Cadillac XLR was a successful interpretation of the Evoq Concept and was built in Bowling Green, Kentucky, on the same assembly line as the Corvette (GM Media).

the SRX. John Phillips stated, "Its engine—from idle to 6000 rpm—is smoother, silkier and more refined than any Detroit-built V-8 I can recall." Ron Kino wrote bluntly, "Cadillac has delivered a knockout hauler of its own. The SRX is not an SUV—just look at it in profile—but rather a CTS wagon with some balls." Csaba Csere wrote, "The Caddy's performance is just a few ticks behind that of the class-leading Infiniti FX45, and the SRX has excellent road manners without beating its occupants with a harsh ride."[10] Looking strictly at the performance numbers, the editors recorded a 0–60 mph time of 6.6 seconds, a standing quarter-mile in 15.0 seconds at 94 mph, and a top speed of 144 mph.

The magazine performed an extended road test of a 2005 SRX and published the findings in the September 2005 issue. The SRX had 4000 miles on the odometer when the editors planned a road trip from Ann Arbor, Michigan, to Boston, Massachusetts, and back. The trip did not go well. At a stop in New York, the SRX failed to restart after repeated attempts. A Cadillac Onstar service technician was consulted by phone, who recommended a curious ignition starting procedure, which proved not to work. Finally the battery was disconnected and reconnected. The SRX started and the editors were on their way, but the problem arose again

The 2004 SRX crossover was Cadillac's first sport utility vehicle and was powered by the RWD Northstar V-8 (GM Media).

in Boston. The problem was diagnosed to lie with the ECM, which had to be replaced. The good news came in the form of increased performance at 40,000 miles compared to their original test of the SRX in 2004. Braking and skidpad performance also improved. When it came time to return the SRX to Cadillac, the vehicle was deemed one of the finest Cadillacs *Car & Driver* had ever tested: "[T]he SRX proved to be reliable and completely competent SUV for our various and often demanding needs and a true performer in rain, shine, sleet, or snow."[11] The last production year of the SRX with available Northstar V-8 was 2009. The next generation SRX was powered by V-6 engines.

4

The Supercharged Northstar V-8, XLR-V and STS-V

Engineering and Development

Two years prior to full production of the Northstar V-8 for installation in the Allanté, talks were already underway to dramatically boost horsepower for GM's most sophisticated engine, still in development. One afternoon in October 1991, Greg Prior was called into the office of Cadillac assistant chief engineer Max Freeman. Prior had been on the Northstar engine program since June of that year, but he was a veteran of General Motors. Prior joined GM in 1979 to work at Buick, initially to work on engine cooling and vehicle aerodynamics with respect to engine cooling. He also spent time working at Oldsmobile and then at Pontiac on various engine projects.

When Prior entered Freeman's office at Cadillac's Clark Street facility, Prior's boss Phil Brooks was also there. Brooks was about to hand Prior the most rewarding and exciting engine project of his career. Prior was told he was to initiate a supercharged Northstar development program, and Brooks explained why. After the Northstar was introduced in the Allanté, it would be rolled out into the Seville, Eldorado and DeVille, and some differentiation for the Allanté would be necessary. As it would eventually turn out, the supercharged Northstar would not be installed in the Allanté, but a new, still-to-be-conceived Cadillac sports car that would be an order of magnitude above the Allanté in every way. In addition, the supercharged Northstar would also undergo an almost total redesign as it was reconfigured to a rear-wheel drive application. These changes would not appear until later. At the time this meeting took place, a supercharged Northstar V-8 was to be for front-wheel drive application.

Brooks also informed Prior that there could be no hood blisters to clear the supercharger or its plumbing; the SC Northstar had to be able to be installed in any Cadillac model without the need for a unique hood. Prior stated that would be a demanding requirement to achieve. Supercharged engines in practically every case required an intercooler that would further elevate the supercharger. Meeting the stock hood requirement would be very challenging. Brooks piled on the misery by saying work on the supercharged Northstar had to be done apart from his daily production engine duties; essentially Prior and a handful of engineers he would pick would have to work after hours on the project.

In his after-work hours, Prior initiated a differentiation study for a supercharged Northstar V-8 to be installed in the Allanté. Engine envelope drawings were produced within the Allanté engine compartment and under its hood line. Calculations were made using existing Northstar spec-

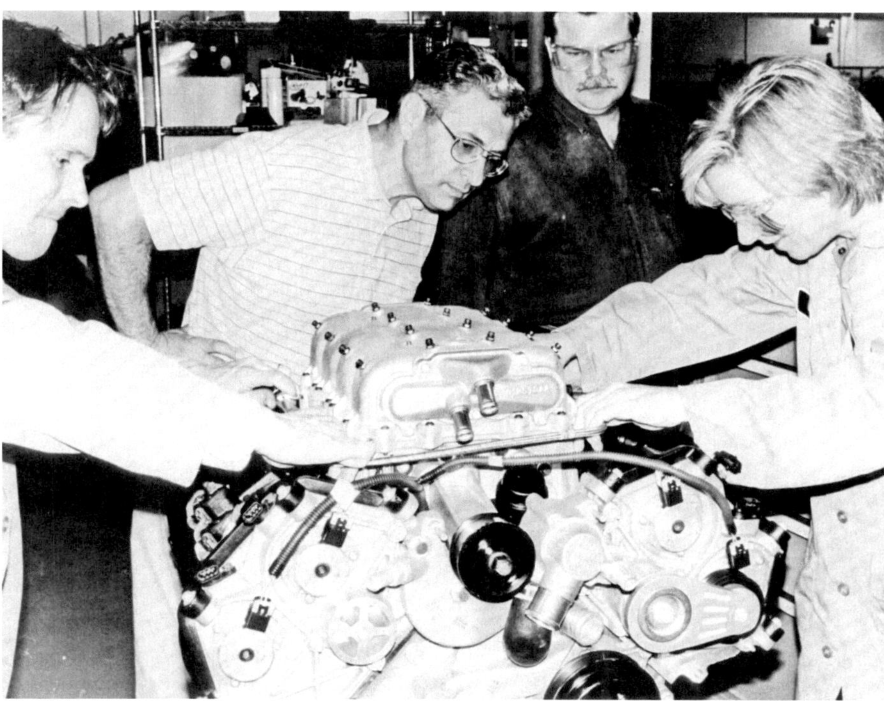

This rare photograph shows the first prototype of the Northstar Supercharged (SC) nearing final assembly (GM Media).

ifications and fuel-air flow, and the goal was established for 330 horsepower with 390 lbs.-ft. of torque. Layout drawings were produced over the next several months that showed the unique intake manifold, aftermarket supercharger and necessarily unique accessory drive to accommodate the supercharger. An intercooler was out of the question, and Prior had reservations about producing a supercharged Northstar V-8 without one. Nevertheless, the low priority of the project—essentially conducting the program as merely experimental—permitted only several hours of work a day on the SC Northstar. At this pace, it would take a year and a half before there would be a running engine.

The Evoq Concept Car

Cadillac has always viewed its striking concept cars as a portent of offerings to come. These cars have been a means of unveiling emerging technology developed under the direction of Cadillac while having an unmistakable aesthetic that would be thrilling to see on the road. Today, Cadillac will sometimes invest millions of dollars in design, engineering and technology development in a vehicle with the intent of integrating as much of it into its production cars as market forces and consumer reaction allow. In fact, many of the features and styling cues have already been targeted for future Cadillac models by the time the concept cars hit the auto show circuit.

Cadillac's foray into concept cars goes back the early 1950s. The newly named Motorama opened in 1953, and this provided the perfect venue for Cadillac to display its line of cars and show off the Le Mans convertible. Compared to its production convertible, the Le Mans was nearly eight inches lower and its fiberglass body removed 400 pounds from its weight. Also at the Motorama that year was the Orleans four-door pillarless hardtop concept; the doors on the Orleans opened in mirror fashion. In 1955, Cadillac exhibited the Eldorado Brougham at Motoramas in New York, Miami, Los Angeles, San Francisco and Boston. This concept car displayed numerous features that would become standard or optional in many other brands in the decades following. These included air suspension, automatic preferred position seat (known as "memory seat" today), self-opening and -closing trunk, and the pillarless four-door design.

Harley Earl's Advanced Styling Studio took a breather for a couple of years, but he was soon back at the board with his talented designers to begin working on a jet aircraft-inspired design. Cadillac for its part pursued new technologies both fanciful and possible for production. The car that emerged was the Cyclone. This was the quintessential show car, from its pinpoint-sharp bullet-shaped two nose cones to the clear dome canopy back to the Cadillac design-inspired fins. The hinged canopy swung up and backward and the doors moved out from the body, then back on tracks for the driver and passenger to enter or exit. The Cyclone had an accident avoidance radar system with proximity sensors mounted in the two nosecones that could detect an object in the road ahead, as well as the distance and stopping distance displayed in real time. The car had a front V-8 engine with rear transaxle for better weight distribution. Visitors to the Motorama, however, were more dazzled by the Cyclone's stunning looks than its technological marvels.

Numerous other striking Cadillac concept cars were designed and displayed during the 1970s and the 1980s. These cars perpetuated the aura of technical innovation, hoped-for styling and unabashed automotive excitement. During this period, Cadillac sales were declining in the face of competition primarily from Lexus, but also from BMW and Mercedes. The right-sized Eldorado and Seville did well in the marketplace, but Cadillac general manager John Smith realized GM's luxury brand needed a complete makeover. He felt, in fact, Cadillac had to make a paradigm shift in terms of design and engineering if it was to successfully compete against the Japanese and European luxury brands.

In 1997, Smith contacted Wayne Cherry, GM's vice president of design, and discussed his vision for Cadillac. Smith was going to give a presentation to top national dealers that summer and wanted Cherry to come up with a concept that would show the direction Cadillac could take in the near future. Cherry put his best designers onto the task. Various designs were created, then refined in a successful attempt to draw on Cadillac's legacy of offering handsome, enduring design while pushing the aesthetic envelope. Smith received an overwhelming response from the dealers who saw the striking rendering, and he knew he was on to something. He continued to meet with Cherry, as well as Peter Levin, director of strategic marketing for Cadillac. By February 1998, Smith's small team had ready a comprehensive presentation for the future design direction for Cadillac to show the company's North American strategy board. The presentation was a stunning success and met with the board's approval.

The next step was to get the funding for the design and construction of a concept car that embraced this new design philosophy, which became known at Cadillac as Art & Science. This car would not be a vision of what might come from Cadillac, but what was indeed going to come from Cadillac. The paradigm shift was already underway at Cadillac and this started happening very quickly. Wayne Cherry's team drew their design inspiration from a number of industrial design icons and new military aircraft—specifically the F-117 stealth fighter. A front-engine two-seater was chosen for the car's configuration. Renderings gave way to models in various scales as the design studio grappled with the car's aesthetic basis, and then on to full-size clay bucks. Kip Wasenko headed up the small design team of Scott Wassell and Chip Thole. The car was given the name Evoq. As the design evolved, Cadillac engineers met with GM Powertrain to discuss the powerplant and driveline. The Northstar V-8 was designed for front-wheel drive, but the Evoq was to be rear-wheel drive. The engine

The Northstar SC with dress cover removed reveals the design of the low-profile supercharger and the routing of supercharged intake. Note the close-coupled catalysts for improved emissions (GM Media).

was envisioned for future Cadillac models having rear-wheel drive, and this would require re-engineering much of the engine while retaining its 32-valve DOHC design. Cadillac went even further and decided for the first time to employ supercharging to dramatically boost the Northstar V-8's output. Another radical departure seen on Evoq was to be a retractable hardtop—this concept car would be no ragtop.

The Evoq was a pivotal concept vehicle for Cadillac to undertake. It was not initiated as simply a showcar in the same mold as the Cyclone, which really had no future as a production car. The Evoq was designed within the realm of production possibility. John Zinser was chief engineer of Premium V Engines at General Motors when the Evoq concept was initiated, and Prior credits Zinser with supporting the engine program to make the concept a fully running reality.

The Evoq could be the platform for the experimental supercharged Northstar V-8. Prior remembers going to Zinser with his outline of the program and what it would require in terms of engineering assets, how long it would take to get running, what level of performance could be achieved, and other matters related to the engine and vehicle. Zinser asked Prior several pointed questions to satisfy his need to make sure it could be realized and within budget. Satisfied with the Prior's answers, Zinser got behind the program one hundred percent. This engine would reinforce the styling statement the Evoq would make and offer a performance statement equal to the concept car's striking looks. Zinser very much liked the idea of a future supercharged Cadillac.

Developing a Running Prototype

The prototype supercharged Cadillac Northstar V-8 for the Evoq was designed at the division's Clark Street location. The preliminary work done on the SC Northstar for the Allanté was a natural segue to work on the Evoq's engine. The supercharger employed was initially an off-the-shelf unit GM used on its production 3.8 liter V-6 engine. This was an Eaton 90-cubic-inch supercharger and was undersized for the 4.6 liter Northstar application. Later during this engine's development, the engine used the longer 112-cubic-inch rotors from Eaton. Prior put Jim Cremonesi to the task of designing the rotating and reciprocating parts. Cremonesi also handled the lubrication system for this engine, and he also designed a cast 9.0 compression ratio piston. Jeff Pigott designed the belt-driven accessory drive that would incorporate the supercharger. When the Allanté model was canceled, Prior focused on the Evoq rear-wheel configuration for the supercharged Northstar V-8.

The prototype engine blocks were poured at Process Foundry in Romulus, Michigan, and the cylinder heads were cast at the Montupet Foundry in Rivierre Beadette, Quebec, Canada. The cylinder blocks and heads were machined by Linamar in Guelph, Ontario, Canada. This engine had the unique design of a rear air inlet to the supercharger. This first engine was assembled at the Clark Street facility as the machined parts were delivered. Dynamometer time was always at a premium, with so many planned production engines under development testing. Prior had the first running supercharged Northstar in 198 days from the start of the project. However, one of the early tests did not go as planned. In an attempt to lower the intake air charge so as to boost the spark advance and improve the engine's torque, dry ice was placed on top of the intake manifold, which was above the supercharger.

The test cell was an eerie sight with dry ice vapor rolling off the top of the engine, which was running close to its redline, and the exhaust manifolds glowing bright red. Midway through the power run, there were three loud bangs. An engineer hit the E-stop button to stop the engine test. Upon disassembly it was discovered that the dry ice had shrunk the rotor case into the spinning rotors.

The Evoq would indeed be a running concept car and another engine was built for the test mule of this car. It was a stretched Corvette, actually an old development car nicknamed "the Rat" for reasons unknown. This was used as a calibration vehicle while the Evoq body was being built by Metalcrafters in California. The stretched Corvette was converted by Advanced Automotive Technologies in Rochester Hills, Michigan, to match the wheelbase of the Evoq. A particularly challenging task for Metalcrafters was fabricating the articulating folding hardtop to disappear into a portion of the trunk space. The stowed top gave the Evoq a strikingly sleek look. The finished body was shipped back to Detroit and the show car was painted, a complete drivetrain installed and the interior completed. Cadillac repeatedly tested the folding hardtop so it would work as planned at the January 1999 Detroit Auto Show. *AutoWeek* magazine voted the Evoq the best concept car at the show. The response from show-goers was overwhelmingly positive, and Cadillac moved forward to take the car to the Paris Auto Show and even let journalists drive it at the Mortefontaine test track north of Paris. This was a particularly daring move on the part of Cadillac, as concept cars like the Evoq are very expensive to build. The supercharged Northstar V-8 in the car was also a one-off with no long-term durability testing performed on it. Cadillac took suitable safeguards for the engine by installing a rev limiter, and a Cadillac engineer always went along for the drive with the journalists. The stunning acceleration of the Evoq and the car's amazing handling impressed the collected auto journalists, who wrote very positive profiles of the car.

The initial plans to develop the engine outside of GM were shelved and the program was kept within the corporation. Continuing product improvement on the FWD Northstar resulted in detail enhancements in the engine, while development continued on the RWD naturally aspirated Northstar V-8. In October 2000, Prior was promoted to project manager of the Northstar engine team. On Prior's engineering team for the production supercharged Northstar V-8 project were Jeff Pigott and Jim Cre-

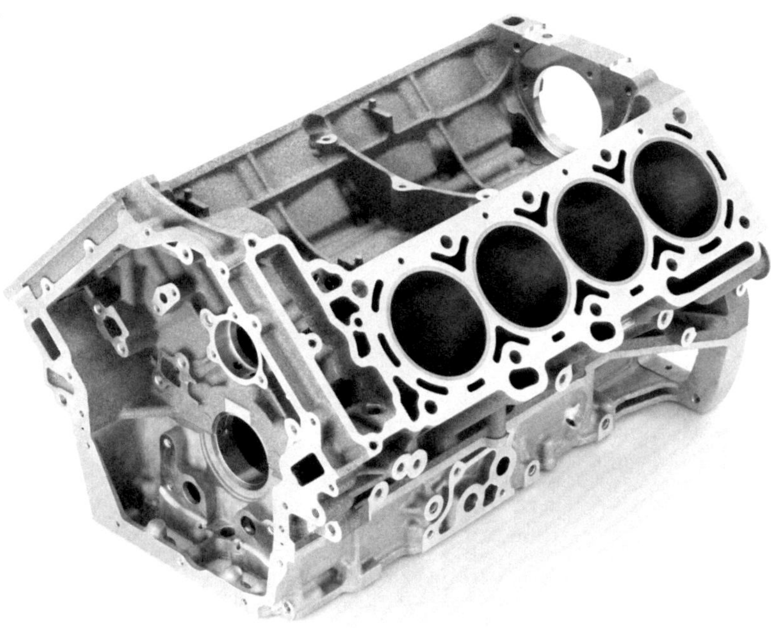

The upper engine block of the Northstar SC was completely different from the naturally aspirated RWD Northstar V-8 (GM Media).

monesi in a part-time capacity. Roxann Bittner had extensive production Northstar engine experience along with her work on the Evoq engine, and she focused her talents on the SC Northstar as well. Also contributing to the SC Northstar program was Dave Kokochak, who had a wealth of engineering experience to add to the program. During 2001, various intercooler designs and configurations, inlet ducts and other engine systems were investigated, along with packaging constraints of the SC Northstar in cars under design development.

For this development engine, displacement was reduced to 4.2 liters. Much of what had been learned from the Evoq supercharged Northstar engine program came to bear on the proposed RWD supercharged Northstar engine. Originally, an output of 420 horsepower was targeted. Then, management upped the horsepower requirement so the engine block was bored out to 91 mm, and this increased the displacement to 4.4 liters, which analysis proved was within the block's safety factor. Additional development with Eaton increased the length of the supercharger rotors and their housing increased the supercharger's displacement to 122 cubic inches.

One of the most challenging aspects of designing the production SC Northstar V-8 was the blower development. The 122-cubic-inch blower required 85 horsepower to turn at its rated speed. This placed a tremendous load on the drive belt, and there were several failures of the belt during tests. Engineers Jeff Pigott and Dave Kokochak worked many additional hours to design a drive belt and related systems to make this durable and reliable.

There were other vexing problems that were more obscure and took efforts to locate and resolve. In one of the early development cars, engineers detected a low-level buzzing sound coming from the engine compartment while the car was idling. Using an acoustic probe, they isolated the sound and learned it was coming from the oil cooler. It was removed and disassembled and they determined it was the piston check balls bouncing off their seats from the oil pump pressure pulses. A revision in the spring rate solved the noise problem.

Engine output was boosted with a switch to Laminova intercoolers, which lowered charge temperature, and added-in engine sealing. This also reduced supercharger whine by damping the outlet pulses. A key element of this was the design of the induction system, designed by Bittner working closely with analysis engineer Anbu Anbarasu to optimize the induction tubes in the confined space behind the engine near the vehicle's firewall.

Dyno technician Jeff Hopper first started the engine in the dynamometer cell on April 26 and development began in earnest. Before long the 4.2L, 112-cubic-inch supercharger versions were producing 420 HP. After the move to 4.4L displacement and 122-cubic-inch supercharger rotors, 440 HP was achieved. After extensive development the engine produced an SAE rating of 469 HP at 6,400 rpm and 439 ft.-lb. at 3,900 rpm in STSV applications and 444 HP at 6,400 rpm and 414 ft.-lb. at 3,900 rpm in XLRV applications. The engine ran the grueling 200-hour GED durability cycle successfully.

From Evoq to XLR

While the supercharged Northstar V-8 and design and development of the Evoq evolved more or less concurrently, the production car based on the Evoq would be available with both the normally aspirated front engine-RWD Northstar V-8 and the Northstar SC V-8. Again, the design mandate did not permit a unique hood for the supercharged Northstar to be installed in the production car. In the end, the XLR-V did receive the requisite but subtle hood bulge. As with other all-new vehicles, Cadillac's flagship production sportscar was given an alphanumeric designation; the XLR moniker would not appear until much later in the car's design and development. For the sake of convenience, I will refer to this entire history as the development of the XLR. General Motors has specific new vehicle design and development milestones. The very first is the initiation of the architecture studies, or ASI. For the XLR, the ASI was initiated in February 1999. Because of the high-performance nature of this Cadillac, the XLR would share some aspects with the 6th generation Corvette, despite the fact the Cadillac would have an completely different engine and transmission driveline.

The first task was to incorporate the fantastic appearance of the Evoq into the XLR as closely as aerodynamics, government regulations, production requirements and cost would allow. Tom Peters, who had been with GM since the early 1980s, would be the design chief for the XLR. The production car would have a shorter wheelbase, and the car's doors would be significantly shorter than on the Evoq. The design evolution of the XLR took form in full-size clay bucks and clay scale models. A design driver was the quest for low drag coefficient. For the XLR, the goal was a Cd of 0.31. The radical planes and sharp edges of the Evoq made this a challenging number to achieve in the production design. The rear window surface would be more angled, the roof sail panels, as they are called, were altered from the concept car, and the front-end details such as the grille design, front bumper, headlights and air intake were refined to help improve the Cd. Other subtle changes to the wheel well arches, the mirrors, rear deck surface and even the rear end itself incrementally improved the number. Undercarriage protrusions would be the responsibility of body and chassis engineering, but these were always a consideration in the overall effort to minimize drag.

The combustion chamber of the Northstar SC differed from that of the standard Northstar V-8 and had a lower compression ratio (GM Media).

Another aspect of the design considered during this phase was drag and downward pressure as well as lift. The XLR had to be completely stable at its top speed without the addition of exaggerated spoilers that would increase vehicle drag and affect the desired aesthetic. Cadillac looked at some very successful older high-performance cars that had achieved this goal, such as the Ferrari 365 GTB/4 from the early 1970s, which was capable of achieving 170 miles per hour and had no add-on spoilers of any kind.

As the body was being refined, the body structure was also undergoing design engineering. The XLR would employ what GM would call the "performance car architecture."[1] The C6 Corvette and the Cadillac XLR would share much of this architecture, although they were not identical. Both cars would have the identical wheelbase of 105.7 inches. If the XLR had had a proprietary body/chassis structure, the cost would have been prohibitive for what would be a limited production car. Computer 3-D modeling of all vehicle structure also permitted finite element analysis of each component and the structure as a whole to ensure absolute rigidity and crash survivability to protect occupants. It featured a steel hydroformed perimeter frame. Specific aluminum alloy castings and machined parts were employed extensively throughout the body. However, it was the emergence of carbon fiber that allowed significant weight savings in an effort to achieve the goal of weight below 3800 pounds. The strong, lightweight material was used exclusively for interior and especially exterior panels.

During this phase of design engineering, considerable effort was devoted to the design of the articulated stowable hardtop. Cadillac did not want a soft top for the XLR and had many good reasons for that in the Allanté. The demands on such a design necessitated turning to a specialist in the design and manufacture of such automotive equipment. The XLR chief engineer, Dave Leone, had also worked on the Allanté, and did not want to revisit the prospect of dealing with sealing issues and durability with a soft top.

Two aftermarket suppliers were considered in this quest. The first was Dura, a domestic supplier of tops, primarily of the soft top configuration, and the second was Car Top Systems (CTS) of Germany. CTS had experience in the design of folding hardtop systems, and when Cadillac approached the company, it was working on the new folding hardtop design for the next generation Mercedes-Benz SL.

Cadillac investigated several design configurations to permit folding of the hardtop and the hinging and articulation of the trunk lid. It would have been ideal to have the trunk lid hinge at the bottom edge and open rearward to permit stowing of the top. However, the rear-end design of the trunk lid precluded this approach. Design meetings at Cadillac and between Cadillac and CTS resulted in a different design approach. The trunk lid would have to open in a conventional manner, then articulated links would lift up the trunk lid to a considerable height to permit the folding hardtop to nest clamshell-like and then stop in the trunk area before the trunk lid would then descend to the closed and locked position.

There was an added complexity to the system that involved the proper stowing of the rear quarter windows. These small windows could not simply lower into the bodywork as they do with most convertibles. The original vehicle architecture prevented this possibility. These windows would have to fold inward during the lowering of the hardtop and would actually be sandwiched between the folded rear window and hardtop as it was being stowed. The design engineering of the XLR folding hardtop was practically a program in itself. The top had to be absolutely wind- and watertight, and it had to remain so for years. The mechanisms to lower and raise the top had to be supremely reliable. Design changes to the top and its mechanisms had to be coordinated between Cadillac and CTS. In addition, the software to permit the crucial timing of all these events took months to develop and debug. The hydraulic cylinders to accomplish this were unique to the XLR, and the trunk latching system proved problematic but was finally resolved.

The XLR folding top was subjected to the same durability testing as all other systems of the car. Design and manufacturing tolerances had to be kept to ensure proper sealing over the life of the car. Prototypes were subjected to 30,000 cycles—far more than would be experienced by any owner. A folding hardtop, however, was the only possible consideration for a high-profile and high-speed sports car like the Cadillac XLR.

The XLR underwent several phases in vehicle development; the three principal phases were known as Alpha, Beta and Gamma. These devel-

Significant engineering went into the design of the supercharger with integral intercooler of the Northstar SC (GM Media).

opment vehicles were built at General Motors pre-build center in Michigan, essentially GM's "skunkworks." The earliest prototypes, or test mules, as they are known, were Corvettes with Northstar drivetrain with either the naturally aspirated Northstar V-8 or the Northstar SC. The Beta vehicles employed the current XLR bodywork, and each such vehicle was built at a cost of roughly half a million dollars.

These cars were tested in a variety of places in North America and in Europe. Earliest and subsequent tests were conducted at the GM Milford (Michigan) Proving Grounds. They were also tested at GM Desert Proving Ground in Mesa, Arizona. Everyday driving conditions on public roads required the use of camouflaged bodywork using added body panels and visually altering paint schemes. Later in the vehicle development program, the vehicles were driven from the manufacturing plant in Bowling Green to Indianapolis and other locations around the United States. Cold weather testing was also conducted during the winter months in Kinross, Michigan, in the state's Upper Peninsula at a former Air Force base. The car was driven both in snow and on glare-ice surfaces to evaluate traction control, anti-lock braking, and overall handling in these conditions. Cadillac would further refine its proprietary StabiliTrak active handling system for the XLR.

Some of the most aggressive and revealing testing of XLR preproduction cars took place at the famed Nürburgring circuit 60 miles southwest of Cologne, Germany. Designed and constructed in the 1920s as a premier European race track, decades later it became a desired vehicle development track. It was here Cadillac engineers would wring out the XLR to expose any of the car's weaknesses in handling, braking, steering and other areas. The 14.2-mile course is very demanding, as it should be, and many of the turns and undulating surfaces can literally throw a car off balance. Both NA and SC Northstar V-8 XLR cars were tested here. Since the XLR would also be sold in Europe, some engineering aspects had to be considered for, say, German drivers who would drive the car at its governed maximum of 155 miles per hour for extended periods of time. One of these was the need for a power steering fluid cooler, and these were validated both at Nürburgring and on the Autobahn.

Due to the limited production nature of the Northstar V-8 SC, each engine was hand-built at GM Powertrain's Performance Build Center (PBC) in Wixom, Michigan. Before establishing the Performance Build

Center, a team from GM Powertrain traveled to specialist professional racing teams in the United States and their shops to study the building of racing engines, and they also traveled to Europe to low-volume car builders and studied their manufacturing processes to establish the best practices for the GM Performance Build Center.

Each Northstar V-8 SC built at the Wixom PBC was assembled by one engine assembly technician from start to finish. The assembler selected the engine block and other main components from stock and each part was entered into a computer so the specific parts could be tracked to a particular engine assembly. The engine block was first bolted to a movable assembly stand which would move from station to station. As the engine builder completed each assembly step at one station, he would move his engine to the next station to perform the next assembly step. This would leave the last assembly station open for the next engine assembler. There were approximately 15 assembly stations for the Northstar V-8 SC. Upon completion of the engine assembly, a series of quality checks were performed, apart from the checking of bolt torque specifications during assembly. After these quality checks, the assembler signed off on the engine that the checks had been performed. The engines were then moved to a hot test area where they were bolted to a test stand and a 20-minute computerized test was conducted and their performance parameters confirmed. After cooldown, the engine was crated and then shipped to the Cadillac assembly plant, where either the XLR-V or the STS-V would have its specific engine installed. The Performance Build Center has a total performance engine assembly of roughly 15,000 engines per year for various GM automotive divisions.

"This process brings a higher level of quality, because each builder is personally involved in *every* aspect of the assembly," said Performance Build Center site manager Timothy Schag.[2] The team members responsible for assembling the Northstar V-8 SC were chosen from GM's experimental engine laboratory in Pontiac, Michigan, for the experience in building individual test engines.

The SC Northstar was now set to be installed in the XLR-V and an even more powerful version of it would be installed in the STS-V and offered first for the 2006 model year. The XLR-V version was ultimately rated at 444 horsepower and the STS-V engine was rated at an impressive 469 horsepower.

Design of the Northstar V-8 SC

The structural design of the Northstar V-8 SC was based on the second generation longitudinal rear wheel drive (RWD) Northstar V-8 that was introduced in the 2004 model year. The Northstar V-8 SC had a displacement of 4.4L with a bore and stroke of 91mm X 84mm, compared to the naturally aspirated Northstar V-8, which had a 4.6L displacement with a bore and stroke of 93mm X 84mm. Nevertheless, a significant number of parts were unique to the supercharged version, having been specifically designed and strengthened to incorporate the supercharger and specific cooling requirements due to added thermal loads. Specific technologies incorporated in the supercharged Northstar V-8 include precision sand cast aluminum engine block, multi-layer steel head gaskets, heavy-duty oil-cooled pistons, heavy-duty connecting rods, and specially polished

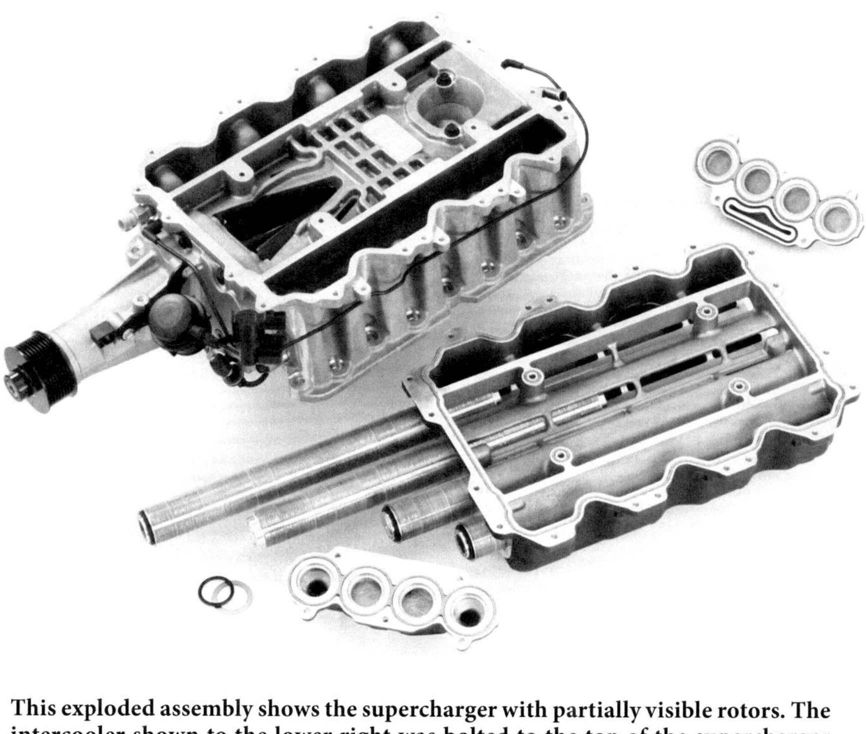

This exploded assembly shows the supercharger with partially visible rotors. The intercooler shown to the lower right was bolted to the top of the supercharger (GM Media).

exhaust ports. Advanced computer modeling using Unigraphics software and finite-element analysis software shortened the design and development of the Northstar V-8 SC.

The engine block comprised two major parts: the upper cylinder case and lower crankcase. The supercharged and NA engines shared the same bore centers, integrally cast chain case, valley mounted starter and Siamesed cylinder bores with cast-in-place iron liners. The cylinder case was precision sand cast of 319 aluminum alloy. The supercharged engine used the same lower crankcase as the NA Northstar. This was a squeeze-cast aluminum casting of ASTM B85 alloy SC84A. The coolant passages in the SC engine block were different from those in the NA engine block. Greater coolant flow was required due to the higher thermal loads imposed by the supercharger. This was achieved by optimizing the coolant path around the cylinder bores. An additional change was the addition of a cast in the oil galley to provide additional crankcase oil through nozzles at the bottom of the bores toward the underside of each piston.

The cylinder heads for the supercharged Northstar V-8 had a lower compression ratio of 9.0:1. They were unique in many other ways as well to integrate with the intake system. These heads retained the same valve angle and cam bores as the NA engine. Intake and exhaust port flow was carefully analyzed to reveal that intake flow as established for the NA engine was adequate for the SC engine, but the exhaust port was modified to have a longer septum, and a patented honing and polishing process known as Extrude Hone was applied to these ports. The cylinder head deck height at the combustion chamber was increased. Combustion chamber design was modified slightly. Both intake and exhaust valve seats were copper infiltrated to improve heat transfer on the SC engine, while the NA engine only had this type of seat on the exhaust seat. Cylinder head gaskets are completely unique to the supercharged Northstar. The cylinder heads were cast using the semipermanent mold process, from 319 aluminum alloy.

The roller chain dual overhead camshaft drive used on the second generation NA Northstar V-8 was adopted in its entirety for the supercharged Northstar with subtle changes optimized for the new application. Principally, the flame-hardened nodular iron camshafts employed new profiles developed for the supercharged application on the Northstar. The exhaust duration profile was increased and the intake duration correspondingly changed to improve the SC engine's breathing; this was determined first through computer modeling and later refined from dynamometer testing. The intake and exhaust valves themselves were virtually unchanged from the NA engine application. The Variable valve timing (VVT) developed for the Northstar V-8 NA was employed for the supercharged application, but incorporated a new specific computer program optimized for the SC. Cadillac and GM Powertrain discovered the VVT on the supercharged Northstar provided even more dramatic performance improvement because of the dual overhead cam system.

Variable valve timing, described in more detail in the chapter devoted to the second generation Northstar V-8, was an engine technology developed for use across the range of engines built by GM, but it was a significant development when used in the Northstar V-8 SC. The VVT permitted separate cam timing that could be individually advanced or retarded depending on idle, partial load and full-throttle acceleration.

Changes to the rotating and reciprocating parts of the Northstar V-8 NA were required for the supercharged Northstar. A different, heavier-duty 9.0:1 piston for the engine's 91mm bore was designed to sustain the higher combustion loads, although having a full point lower compression. The piston pin diameter was increased from 23mm to 24mm to reduce loading on the piston. More significant were the piston oil cooler jets positioned in each cylinder bore to provide constant-pressure oil to spray the bottom of each piston at the bottom of its stroke. The connecting rod was modified over the standard rod with special heat-treating that improved fatigue strength 13 percent. The main and rod bearing surfaces were different to increase oil film thickness for the higher combustion loads.

The forged, micro-alloyed steel crankshaft with rolled journal fillets was carried over from the higher compression naturally aspirated Northstar. Its durability was well within the performance parameters of the supercharged application, but subtle changes were needed to crankshaft weights to account for the changed pistons and connecting rods.

The supercharger was designed to be part of an induction module that also combined the intercooler and intake manifold. The requirements laid down at the start of the Northstar V-8 SC program were:

- High airflow capability to enable the output target to be met. The original target was 400g/sec at rated engine speed.
- High charge density was required. Both a low supercharger delta T (i.e., temperature rise across the supercharger) and an efficient intercooler

system for a high IC delta T were required. The target for the intercooler system was at least 40 degrees Centigrade delta T under rated conditions.

- Excellent reliability, even under extended boosted operation, and varying intercooler temperatures.
- Refined Noise, Vibration and Harshness (NVH) characteristics.
- Efficient use of underhood space.[3]

Development of the supercharged Northstar V-8 for Evoq revealed the underhood limitations of that concept and forecast similar issues for production Cadillacs. The compact, DOHC design of the Northstar made designing a low-profile supercharged induction system one of the most challenging engineering projects done at GM Powertrain. Another constraint on modifying the vehicle hood to allow for this high-performance application was the forward and downward visibility for the driver. Much of the experience derived from the Evoq engine program was brought to bear on the production Northstar V-8 SC. The design of the supercharger, intercooler and intake manifold induction module was so significant, it was patented. The reduction in height of this module achieved by the outer wall of the supercharger housing was shared with the inner wall of the intake manifold port. This also helped to maintain supercharger bore cylindrical tolerance. The intercooler tubes were at the very top of the module. The supercharger rotors would push the intake air upward through and around the intercooler tubes and the cooled air charge would then travel through the intake manifold passages downward toward the intake ports of the cylinder heads.

The low-volume production of the supercharged Northstar precluded all new supercharger component tooling, including the dies for the rotors, hobbing equipment and new rotor bore machining equipment. In particular, the tooling for larger diameter extruded rotors to achieve the needed flow was prohibitive. The tight space between the DOHC banks was also a constraint on larger rotors. It was decided to employ existing rotor and supercharger machine tooling, and simply manufacture longer rotors to achieve the desired cubic feet per minute of air flow.

The new production rotors were precise mirror images of each other and were press-fit onto steel shafts. The rotor and shaft assembly was supported at the front with ball bearings between rotor gears and front of the rotors and the bearings were lubricated and cooled with synthetic lubricant within the front rotor housing. The shafts were supported at the rear

Each Northstar SC was assembled from start to finish by a single, specially selected and trained engine assembly technician at GM Powertrain's Performance Build Center in Wixom, Michigan (GM Media).

by maintenance-free needle bearings. The rotor gears were driven off the power shaft of the drive pulley front cover assembly as part of the accessory drive serpentine belt. The entire supercharger module was assembled on a new dedicated assembly line at a GM Powertrain division and then shipped to the GM Performance Build Center.

GM Powertrain carefully evaluated air intake even before it entered the supercharger. Computational Fluid Dynamics (CFD) was employed in the design of the air intake system as it had been done for the cylinder heads and supercharger module. The air intake plenums and air cleaner housing were different for the Northstar V-8 SC in the STS-V and the XLR-V.

As vital as the supercharger module was to the engine, the exhaust manifolds and exhaust system were also closely studied to ensure the exhaust flowed as efficiently as the intake. Unigraphics software was employed to study exhaust flow, and heat concentrations in the manifold design. Attention was paid to close cylinder head exhaust port to exhaust manifold alignment. With a high-performance application like this engine, the catalytic converters, or mini-cats, were close-coupled to the exhaust manifolds to ensure quick light-off and continued effective emissions reduction with a minimum of exhaust restriction. The exhaust manifolds for the XLR-V and the STS-V Northstar V-8s were different because of underhood environments and exhaust routing, since the unibody construction differed for each car. The exhaust manifolds were cast from high silicon/molybdenum ferritic nodular iron using green sand molds.

The Northstar V-8 SC Engine Management System (EMS) drew from the control system development for the naturally aspirated second generation RWD Northstar V-8. Despite decades of improved emissions, legislation to reduce them further seems to never plateau or reach a practical limit. Sophisticated EMS and advances such as VVT make this advancement in emissions possible. Emission controls such as Exhaust Gas Recirculation (EGR) and Air Injection Reaction (AIR) were not required on the supercharged Northstar engine. (FWD Northstar V-8 did use AIR starting in 2000 because they did not employ VVT.) At the same time, latest generation EMS permitted uncommonly smooth idle, plus improvement in the vehicle's cruise control and traction control. The EMS also manages all vehicle displays and other readouts for the driver. The main EMS also monitors other electronic systems within the vehicle.

The moment air enters the intake plenum, the EMS is monitoring several factors, including Electronic Throttle Control (ETC). From there, the two visibly prominent (with engine dress cover removed) intake tubes snake around the left and right side of the SCM to the acoustic silencers, and then to the rear intake of the supercharger and the 80mm diameter throttle body plate. The throttle assembly was mounted to the SCM inlet adapter. The fuel injection system was of a conventional design employing fuel rails on the left and right of the SCM with four injectors on each rail. The Engine Control Module performed the precise time of fuel delivery and ignition.

The Northstar V-8 SC lubrication system was closely based on the naturally aspirated RWD Northstar V-8, but with changes. Among these were the previously mentioned piston oil cooling system, additional oil temperature sensors to permit feedback to the VVT and boost trim systems under high speed and load conditions, and additional capability to have vehicles perform on racetrack conditions for the V series XLR and STS without vehicle modification. Lengthy development was necessary to achieve this. A dry sump system was considered and ruled out due to noise, expense, size and complexity. GM Powertrain and Cadillac chose

The Cadillac STS-V powered by the Northstar SC V-8 was introduced in 2006. Its rather conservative looks belied its amazing acceleration and top speed (GM Media).

to make specific changes to the oil pan area, the oil pickup tube, and the oil cooling circuit designed specifically for the XLR-V and the STS-V to achieve the requirements of lubrication and oil cooling in these vehicles. With so many rotating and reciprocating parts in the DOHC Northstar V-8 SC, nothing could be overlooked. In other words, adequate lubrication under all conditions had to be provided even if the V versions of the XLR and STS were raced on the track. Cost-effective means were found to boost oil flow and dispersion throughout the oil lubrication circuit. Changes were made to the size of the oil passages in the oil pump, the relief valve was increased in size, and its passages were carefully designed to minimize noise and oil aeration. The oil filter itself for the V Northstars was larger and had higher flow capacity than the regular Northstar V-8. The Northstar V-8 SC for the XLR-V differed from that in the STS-V in having a different and shallower oil pan, oil pickup tube and oil filter adapter.

The engine cooling system for the Northstar V-8 SC also had unique requirements. Computational Fluid Dynamics (CFD) was used to completely model the cooling requirements of this engine. CFD analysis was used to accurately determine the heat transfer of the engine and supercharger module. The same basic cooling flow layout from the Northstar V-8 RWD engine was retained, with specific changes necessary for the supercharged application. The front cover, coolant outlets and thermostat housings were unique in the supercharged application. CFD evaluation determined the size of the passages for the sand-cast components for the SC engine had lower restriction than the die cast components of the NA engine, so the same coolant pump from the NA engine with several unique external parts could be employed for the SC application. The supercharged Northstar V-8 had a separate and dedicated coolant system for the supercharger module and used the same 50/50 ratio of water to coolant. An Intercooler Heat Exchanger (ICHE) was installed in front of the main engine radiator. The lower outlet of the ICHE sent the coolant up to the inlet of the SCM, through the intercooler passages, then back out the front of the intercooler to a return line to the ICHE.

The accessory drive systems on today's automotive engines are often overlooked by those fascinated with the internals of an engine like the supercharged Northstar V-8, but they are a vital system in the engine's proper performance. A specific, dedicated design engineer is often responsible for the accessory drive alone. Power to run the accessory drive serpentine belts comes from the main crankshaft pulley or pulleys. The air conditioning compressor, power steering pump, generator, and coolant pump must all be driven, and on a supercharged Northstar V-8, this was also powered by a serpentine belt with a minimum of 170 degrees of belt contact with the pulley. Due to the engine compartment volume, body structure design and underhood environment, the accessory drives for the XLR-V and STS-V were completely different. Both engines employed three serpentine belts, but the juxtaposition of the driven components and belt tensioners was entirely different.

Within the luxury car market segment, there is a specific portion of the vehicle and engine program devoted to noise, vibration and harshness (NVH). With the Cadillac Northstar V-8 SC and the XLR-V and STS-V it powered, the levels of NVH had to be of the lowest possible order. Cadillac employed Finite Element Method (FEM) through the vehicle program to optimize NVH performance before any prototypes were built. Depending on the parts and their specific function, materials were selected with an eye toward reducing NVH. For example, forged steel was employed in the crankshaft, coupled with critical balancing to reduce vibration. The supercharger presented unique challenges to reduce NVH, particularly inlet and outlet noise and rotor gear noise. Inlet noise was reduced by careful design of the induction silencers which reduced noise 35dBA. Supercharger outlet noise was reduced by the design of large back flow slots in each rotor chamber before opening to the supercharger outlet, which reduced pressure pulsations. A careful balance of exhaust noise to pleasing exhaust note from idle up to redline was rigorously examined. The XLR-V used active mufflers to optimize noise reduction with the lowest possible backpressure. Acoustic dampening materials were employed strategically throughout the vehicles. Cadillac employed acoustic sensor probes to isolate noises coming from the engine and the exhaust system. A full engine-transmission closeout panel was designed for the XLR-V and STS-V to eliminate the open path of noise radiating from the bell housing area. Topside, an engine acoustic cover was designed to further reduce noise.

The high torque and horsepower output of the Northstar V-8 SC required a special RWD transmission. General Motors' GM Powertrain division had been working on such a transmission current with the supercharged Northstar V-8 program. This transmission was the Hydra-Matic 6L80 six-speed transmission. It was designed to be used in the Chevrolet Corvette C6 and the Cadillac STS-V and XLR-V. The 6L80 was actually

The XLR-V was produced from 2006 to 2009, ending concurrently with the standard XLR (GM Media).

a member of a new transmission family, all having six speeds for improved acceleration and fuel economy. This six-speed transmission group was designed to replace the four-speed and five-speed transmissions that had been in production since the 1990s. The first Cadillac to get the 6L80 transmission was the 2006 STS-V, and the XLR-V followed in 2007.

"The STS-V provides the ultimate showcase for the new 6L80 six-speed automatic: the car's supercharged Northstar 4.4L DOHC V-8 develops 440 horsepower at 6400 rpm and 430 lb.-ft. of torque at 3600 rpm," said Jeffrey K. Baran, chief engineer of the six-speed RWD transmission family. "Apart from its ability to handle supercharged Northstar's torque, the STS-V demonstrates the strong acceleration potential of the new six-speed's wide 6.04 overall gear ratio."[4]

Road Testing the Northstar V-8 SC

The Northstar V-8 had garnered the respect of the mainline automotive magazines and the editors were eager to get their hands on Cadillacs with the supercharged engine. Among the first such magazines was *Road & Track*. In the January 2005 issue, editor Matt Delorenzo was able to go to the General Motors Milford Proving Ground in the fall of 2004 and drive the pre-production 2006 STS-V and the XLR-V. With the STS-V, Cadillac rated the engine's maximum horsepower at 469.

Delorenzo met and spoke with Cadillac's general manager at the time, Jim Taylor, who stated part of Cadillac's turnaround was attributed as much to engineering as aesthetics. "You can generate a lot of interest with the look of a car to signal change and freshness," Taylor told Delorenzo, "but you have to back it up with legitimate hardware. If you don't have no-excuse cars, we wouldn't earn our way back to credibility."[5]

The Milford Proving Ground was the perfect venue to really show the capabilities of the supercharged Northstar V-8 as well as the cars it powered. The editor was able to take the STS-V up to nearly 140 miles per hour before having to brake hard to go into a long sweeping right-hand turn. The six-speed automatic transmission had a manual sequential shift feature. While the car definitely had performance, it was after all a Cadillac and had to also be extremely smooth and drivable on a daily basis. This was the balance Cadillac was striving to achieve with the STS-V. Delorenzo was favorably impressed with the capabilities of the car, while it also retained Cadillac's reputation for luxury in its appointments and accessories.

In the February 2005 issue of *Car & Driver,* editor Csaba Csere reported on his experience with the STS-V. Csere admitted the supercharged Northstar was an impressive piece of engineering, but stated the power output "doesn't exactly set new standards for the class. Nevertheless, the STS-V could achieve a top speed of 165 miles per hour. Power was never the only criteria [*sic*] and fuel economy continued to also be a goal not only of Cadillac but of all automotive manufacturers. The six-speed automatic transmission certainly helped Cadillac achieve impressive gas mileage despite the car's weight of 4300 pounds."

After several years of Northstar V-8 SC production, even *Popular Hot Rodding* took notice of the superb engineering and performance generated by this engine. Editor Steve Dulcich was very impressed with the refinement and eye-opening power of 1.65 horsepower per cubic inch. Even more impressive to Dulcich was the supercharged Northstar V-8's ability to generate 90 percent of its rated peak torque of 430 lb.-ft. at 3,600 anywhere from a mere 2,200 rpm all the way up to 6,000 rpm. This engine's variable valve timing (VVT) and the intercooled supercharger complemented each other and allowed for such dramatic torque and horsepower specification.

"Four-cam VVT is an exceptional performance enabler," said Dave Caldwell, the Northstar V-8 SC development and calibration engineer told *Popular Hot Rodding*, "but it also provides the control flexibility needed for highly advanced NVH and emissions characteristics. The supercharger module and VVT system complement one another, resulting in a genuine luxury and performance engine."[6]

Road & Track was eager to drive the XLR-V to see how it stacked up against the Mercedes-Benz SL55-AMG. Editor John Lamm reported:

> Start the supercharged V-8, drive away smartly and the XLR-V's true nature rises to the surface. Great sounds emanate from the stainless-steel exhaust tips, and there's grunt to go with it. Now is when it feels equivalent to the SL55 as you leave traffic behind. Then the corners begin to weave left-right and tighten up. Does the Cadillac still feel like a Mercedes? No, but that's not necessarily bad. You'll find the American sports car as willing to take on the twisty stuff, but with less of a hard edge than the Mercedes. There's initial understeer, of course, good turn-in and an ability to remain stable without being harsh, plus a solid transition back the other way as the road turns. The XLR-V may not give you the look-at-me-I'm-a-race-driver thrill of the SL55 AMG, but it wouldn't be far behind on a curving road ... and it is arguably a better day-to-day driver.[7]

The STS-V remained in production for four years—from 2006 through 2009. Fewer than 100 units were built in its last year of production, which makes the 2009 STS-V a particularly collectible Cadillac which is certain to go up in value in the future. This was also the last year of production for the XLR and the XLR-V.

The Northstar V-8–powered Eldorado ETC was a perfect blend of style, performance and luxury. This example is from 1999 (GM Media).

The DeVille of the early 2000s was perhaps the least-successful design to be produced by Cadillac. Magazine editors praised the 2001 DeVille for its excellent road manners (GM Media).

This cutaway illustration of the Allanté shows how tightly the Northstar V-8 was packaged under the car's hood (GM Media).

The Northstar V-8 strongly influenced the design engineering of the 4.0 liter DOHC V-8 that powered the Oldsmobile Aurora. This is the 2002 model (GM Media).

For several years, Cadillac raced the twin-turbocharged Northstar-powered Le Mans Prototype—the LMP. Cadillac raced these cars more for image-building than seeking the winner's circle (GM Media).

The XLR was far superior to the Allanté and was a successful production interpretation of the Evoq Concept. It was available with either naturally aspirated or supercharged Northstar V-8 engines (GM Media).

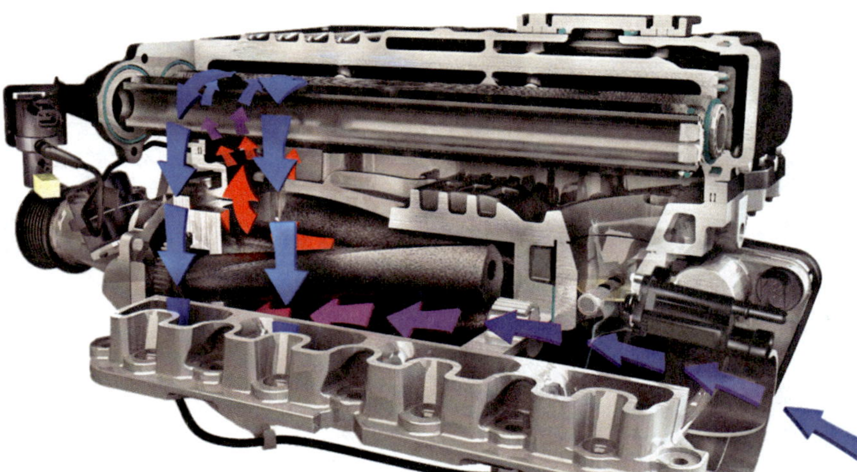

This cutaway illustration shows the air flow and operational components of the Northstar V-8 supercharger (GM Media).

5

The New Multi-cylinder Era

The Northstar XV12 and V-16 OHV Sixteen Concept

The Cadillac division of General Motors and Cadillac enthusiasts around the world have always regarded the V-16 and V-12 cars of the 1930s as a pinnacle in the luxury brand's history. These engines and the cars they powered were conceived in the late 1920s while the American economy was booming and luxury brands like Lincoln, Packard, Duesenberg and Rolls-Royce competed for the wealthy buyers of such cars. The desirability of these cars was enhanced by stunning coachwork so handsome and beautifully finished, people walking down the street would stop and stare as these cars drove by. Even as the Great Depression wore on during the 1930s, Cadillac was dauntless in continuing to market these V-16 and V-12 models, known among classic aficionados as "multi-cylinder" cars due to their having more than eight cylinders. The V-12 and V-16 engines remained in production through the 1937 model year.

In the early 1960s, Cadillac once again looked at the possibility of offering a V-12 engine in its cars. Cadillac engineer Paul Keydel was placed in charge of the new engine program, which was given the name V-Future V-12. It was to be a single overhead camshaft design having 60-degree cylinder banks with an initial displacement of 7.4 liters or roughly 450 cubic inches. The first prototype ran in May of 1963 and it developed 295 horsepower with 418 lb.-ft. of torque. A larger displacement V-12 was designed displacing 8.2 liters or roughly 500 cubic inches. This engine ran in April of 1964 and developed 394 horsepower with over 500 lb.-ft. of torque. These engines did not go into production because, as designed, they could not meet proposed emissions regulations for the mid- to late 1960s.[1]

The magnificent Cadillac Sixteen Concept was the idea of General Motors executive Bob Lutz, who had championed the Dodge Viper when he worked at Chrysler. The V-16 engine used conventional overhead valves but still was capable of producing 1000 horsepower (GM Media).

Jaguar of England began to study a V-12 engine for its sedans and XKE sports car about this time, and it would be designed to meet any and all emissions regulations. The V-12 provided the power desired and the inherent smoothness Jaguar management wanted in its cars. Jaguar had investigated V-12 engines in the early 1950s to be used in its racing cars destined for Le Mans. The cost of the racing program forced Jaguar to withdraw from all forms of road racing and the V-12 engine program was shelved. Jaguar management reviewed the possibility of a street V-12 engine in the late 1960s and the engine program was approved. This design was a two-valve-per-cylinder SOHC design with the engine having 5.3 liter displacement. Prototype engines had a redline of 6500 rpm, deemed adequate for an automobile driven on the street. The first Jaguar to receive this V-12 was the 1971 Series 3 E-Type XKE. This V-12 and several variants went on to power other Jaguars throughout the 1970s and into the early 1980s.[2]

V-12 engines were the standard powerplant configuration for Ferrari and Lamborghini road cars for several decades. Mercedes-Benz had not gone beyond the V-8 in number of cylinders until the late 1980s. BMW kept its straight-six engine in several displacements even in its largest sedan until 1987, when it introduced its first V-12 engine. The two German car manufacturers pursued V-12 engine development and production to offer these engines in their most expensive models for the ultimate in refinement, power, technological prowess, and automotive prestige.

BMW V-12 Engine Offerings

BMW introduced its V-12 engine, code named M70, for its 1988 model year for the 750i and 750iL 7 sedans. The company copied much of the engine architecture and components from the existing M20 SOHC two-valve-per-cylinder straight-six engine that had been in production for years, thus significantly reducing development and production risk by taking advantage of the legacy engineering and reliability of the six-cylinder engine. This 60-degree V-12 engine, the M70, had a 5.0 liter displacement having 300 horsepower with 330 lb.-ft. of torque. BMW kept this engine in production for several years to gain confidence with the engine's design and reliability before increasing its displacement. In 1992, the company introduced two larger displacement variants. The new 5.6 liter version developed 380 horsepower with 410 lb.-ft. of torque. The other engine was a four valve-per-cylinder V-12 with just over 6.0 liter displacement and was practically a racing engine. It was rated at over 600 horsepower at 7400 rpm. This engine was employed in the McLaren F1 and BMW's LM and LMR racing cars.

For 1994, BMW introduced the 750i with available M73 SOHC V-12 engine having 5.4 liter displacement with 320 horsepower and 360 lb.-ft. of torque. This remained BMW's premium engine in its largest sedan for several years, but the company was working on a DOHC four-valve-per-cylinder version having larger displacement. This was the M73, having 6.0 liter displacement and rated at 439 horsepower with 440 lb.-ft. of torque. It remained in production through the 2008 model year. This engine served as the basis for the N74, which was equipped with twin turbochargers and was designed with variable valve timing and variable valve lift. It was rated at 540 horsepower and 550 lb.-ft. of torque.

Mercedes-Benz V-12 Engine Offerings

Mercedes-Benz entered the V-12 engine stakes later than BMW. The first V-12 passenger car engine this company built was the M120 with DOHC and four valves per cylinder. This 6.0 liter engine was initially rated at 408 horsepower at 5200 rpm with 428 lb.-ft. at 3800 rpm. That year the V-12 was offered in the 600 SEL and continued to be offered in this model for the rest of the decade. The power and torque were lowered slightly beginning in 1993. The engine was offered exclusively in the 600 series coupes and sedans and the 600SL (later SL600 roadster). From 2000 through 2002 it was available in the 600SL only.

There were both smaller displacement and larger displacement variants of this V-12 engine built by AMG and offered in limited production cars. There were 5.5 and 5.8 liter displacements versions offered in the CL 55 AMG, CL 58 AMG, CL 63 AMG and CL 65 AMG models. There was also a turbocharged and supercharged version of the 5.5 liter motor and a turbocharged version of the 6.5 liter motor with over 600 horsepower.

Cadillac Considers a Northstar V-12

Cadillac management viewed the V-12 engine offerings from Aston Martin, BMW and Mercedes-Benz as a challenge for engineering supremacy. The V-12 engines in the Ferraris and Lamborghinis were in a separate league and for a different market buyer altogether. However, those exotic Italian V-12 engines did have dual overhead cams and four valves per cylinder as well. At General Motors, the corporation wanted to explore the prospect of a DOHC four-valve-per-cylinder engine—a Northstar V-12. Preliminary design efforts on a Northstar XV12 began in late 1999. This was to be GM's premium engine, over and above the Northstar V-8. It would incorporate a host of new engine technologies the corporation wanted to use, including Displacement on Demand and variable cam phasing, later referred to as Variable valve timing (VVT). It was to be compact in order to fit into as many Cadillac vehicles as possible. At the same time, this engine would incorporate as many existing Northstar components as possible to reduce design, development and manufacturing cost.

GM Powertrain's Steve Kowalk was project manager and placed in charge of the XV12's design and development. One of the key goals of this engine program was packaging—the envelope of the XV12 could not exceed that of GM's existing big-block V-8, which was the 8.1 liter Vortec engine. The engine would not be a 90-degree but a 60-degree V between the cylinder banks. The XV12 was not simply a scaled-up Northstar V-8 having four additional cylinders. If the 4.6 liter Northstar V-8's bore and stroke was applied to a V-12, the displacement would be 6.9 liters. GM wanted a 7.5 liter V-12 in order to compete with the offerings from England and Germany, and to have a unique image. After careful consideration, it was felt a 7.5 liter engine was considered a good balance of image and displacement. The target peak output of this engine would be 750 horsepower with 450 lb.-ft. of torque, naturally aspirated, or roughly 100 horsepower per liter. At the same time, under light load conditions, the engine was to have the fuel economy of a 3.8 liter V-6 engine. The goal was to achieve this using Displacement on Demand, a far more sophisticated, workable and reliable technology than the failed 8–6–4 technology offered by Cadillac in the early 1980s.

"The packaging was probably the biggest challenge we faced," Kowalk stated in 2002, "because from the outset we wanted to fit the V-12 inside the package of a V-8. We focused on keeping the size down to fit as many different types of vehicles as possible, while maximizing displacement, and then using Displacement on Demand to deliver the required power at all times. We also minimized cylinder-bore wall thickness to 7 mm and used a rear cam drive to create a more compact package and enable a lower hoodline."[3]

Specifically, Cadillac was interested in moving the brand beyond the $60,000 Escalade. The plan was to offer a V-12 in the Escalade and in a flagship sedan. This was two years before the Cien Concept surfaced. Looking at all the technical and manufacturing potential problems, Cadillac saw nothing insurmountable technically, but in terms of manufacturing, the challenge would be finding a low-volume production engine builder and in lining up suppliers to provide production parts in limited quantity. The findings from this aspect of the engine program was the driving force behind the eventual creation of the GM Performance Build Center in Wixom, Michigan. The Northstar SC V-8 was built at the Performance Build Center.

GM's Powertrain High Performance Vehicle Group was a key group in the development of the XV12. In addition, the Powertrain Synthesis and Analysis group in Pontiac, Michigan, was involved in the specialized computer modeling of the engine and its virtual operation within the digital realm to optimize the engine's performance in all potential situations before the first part was cast or machined. These high-tech GM facilities permitted better definition of design with greater certainty of actual performance when it came to issue the orders for the first development parts. The XV12 was also meant to be a test bed as well of emerging performance and emissions improving technologies that would find their way into standard vehicle engines built by GM Powertrain.

The XV12 had much the same engine valvetrain geometry as the Northstar V-8. However, the XV12 employed rear chain camshaft drive. Also, this engine had 100mm bore spacing compared to the Northstar V-8's 102mm bore spacing. In addition, the XV12 engine block did not use the same cast-in iron liners but dispensed with the iron liners in favor of Nikasil/Plasma-coated cylinder bores. What was also unique was the design and selection of carbon composite induction manifold. This permitted the complex plenum shapes in a large yet lightweight component. This three-stage variable induction system had tuned primary and secondary plenums that resulted in a flat torque curve. It was a simple and compact design that employed electric variable intake valve actuators that enabled rapid changes in manifold geometry over conventional pneumatic actuators.

Instrumental in the engine's viability in a production vehicle was Displacement on Demand. With the XV12, it was determined valve deactivation using a switchable tappet and fuel deactivation would be used on the right-hand cylinder bank, which allowed the engine to run as a balanced inline six-cylinder. Direct fuel injection using a single centrally located injector in the combustion chamber near the spark plug instead of the intake port (known as port fuel injection) improved power, combustion and emissions. The engine would have one close-coupled catalytic converter on each exhaust manifold to allow quick light-off of the converter and optimum emissions. Cosworth Technologies in England was contracted to provide engineering integration of all the engine's new technologies for the program.

Cadillac was coming up on its 100th anniversary in 2002, and the luxury division wanted to design a concept vehicle that celebrated this milestone in Cadillac history while displaying its new Art & Science philosophy first displayed in the Evoq, Imaj and Vizón concept vehicles. When this concept was in development, it was assumed a Northstar V-8 would power the car, but later it was decided to incorporate the proposed XV12 into the concept car. Instead of the car being designed in Detroit, the task of designing this latest concept would be given to GM's Advanced Design Studio in Birmingham, England. Simon Cox, the lead designer at the studio, along with his other designers, set to work to brainstorm ideas for what the car should look like and whether it should be front engine or mid-engine. As Cadillac had in the past, the designers looked for design inspiration in areas other than automotive, and they turned to stealth aircraft. The planar surfaces of the F-117 Nighthawk and F-22 Raptor stealth fighters provided the starting point, and soon the design studio was blanketed in renderings that would put any Lamborghini to shame. Cox did not have a completely free hand, as the designs were reviewed by GM design chief Wayne Cherry.

It was determined this car, given the name Cien (Spanish for 100), would be a mid-engine high-performance statement. More renderings

The Cien Concept was conceived to celebrate Cadillac 100th anniversary as America's premier luxury brand. Originally planned with a mid-engine Northstar V-8, it ultimately showcased the XV12 concept engine (GM Media).

and clay models followed. The mid-engine permitted a very low hood line, and the car's doors would be upward opening, as with the latest Lamborghini. When the decision was made to employ the XV12 engine in the Cien, Steve Kowalk worked with Simon Cox to integrate the engine in the Cien. Placement of the XV12 helped to determine the Cien's center of mass and the design and packaging of the powertrain. Cherry wanted to retain something of a family resemblance with the previous three concept cars, while Cox pushed for a more curvaceous shape; Cherry almost always won the contest. As the Cien turned out, it was a practically perfect balance of the two design philosophies. From the identifiable Cadillac eggcrate grille openings, sharply creased fender lines all the way to the rear taillights, the sail panels (rear roof pillars), the functional side scoops, minimal rear overhang, and striking blue-tint glass and completely visible engine, the Cien was a design *tour de force.*

The car would be based on a carbon fiber monocoque backbone chassis and the body panels would also be formed from carbon fiber. The XV12 was bolted to a specially built transmission and the car featured race-derived paddle shifters to optimize performance. The Cien came with 19-inch front wheels and 21-inch rear wheels. Technological features included Night Vision, which would help the driver detect potentially dangerous situations beyond the range of visibility in nighttime driving situations, to be conveyed on a heads-up display visible on the steeply sloped windscreen. The car had a digital instrument display with all the vehicle's functions and diagnostics. It also featured Ultrasonic Rear Parking Assist and a Communiport that integrated audio, OnStar, navigation and other applications.

The car was first displayed in Monterey, California. Dr. Fritz Indra, GM Powertrain executive director of advanced engineering, told the press, "Engineers love working on cars that look like this and stylists love having engines like this in their cars. The Northstar XV12 provides a realistic look at what could power an assault on the high-end, premium automotive segment. It showcases a wealth of new technologies under development at GM Powertrain, many of which will eventually find their way into GM engines of all shapes and sizes."[4]

Wayne Cherry, GM's design chief, wanted to make certain he quashed any rumors that this most radical of all Cadillac concepts might be under consideration as a limited-production car. "Most concepts reflect work we're doing here," he told the editors of *Car & Driver,* "but the Cien does

The Cien Concept was designed at GM's Advanced Design studio in England, where the car was also built. Most of the body panels and structure were carbon fiber composite. The XV12 engine is visible through the rear window (GM Media).

not. Don't confuse it with things that we'll produce."[5] The Evoq Concept indeed reflected what eventually went into production as the XLR. The Cien reflected Cadillac's design and engineering prowess to the world; Cadillac was not, however, an exotic car builder like Lamborghini. The Cien made the rounds of the national auto shows and even made a trip across the Atlantic to England, where it was driven before amazed crowds on the Goodwood racetrack.

Particularly unfortunate was the decision by General Motors not to pursue production of the XV12. Rumors circulated for years after the Cien's debut and, in fact, GM did have the Northstar V-12 in development, even releasing photos of the V-12 installed in a Cadillac Escalade test vehicle. XV12 was also intended to go into a new flagship sedan and other possible vehicles. The engine would have been the most expensive engine built by GM and its production would have been very limited. There may have been other issues which contributed to the low-key announcement in 2008 that this engine was not approved for production and that for the

GM Northstar XV12
Concept Engine

The Northstar XV12 was a dual overhead cam design originally conceived to go up against the finest automotive engines of Germany and England. The engine program was canceled before it entered production (GM Media).

foreseeable future, the Northstar V-8 would remain the premium engine in the Cadillac lineup.

The Sixteen and XV16 Engine

The Cien Concept awakened a creative spirit at Cadillac with regard to what was possible in both design and engineering and was the first such concept to embrace the Art & Science design philosophy. This would also be reflected in the Cadillac product line. There was another concept in the works as the Cien made the rounds of the auto shows in America and Europe, and it was inspired by one of the auto industry mavericks—Robert Lutz. Perhaps his most high-profile effort was in the creation and eventual production of the Dodge Viper. On September 1, 2001, Bob Lutz

GM Vice Chairman of Product Development Robert Lutz talks with a GM engineer about the performance of the 750 horsepower XV12 engine installed in the Cadillac Escalade development vehicle at a product development seminar in Santa Barbara, California (GM Media).

was lured to General Motors from his presidency at Chrysler Corporation. His new role at GM was vice-chairman of product development and chairman of GM North America. Lutz had several ideas he wanted to realize at General Motors, and one of them was to see a Cadillac concept car that embraced the legendary reputation of the great V-16–powered cars of the classic era in the 1930s but in a contemporary and cutting-edge technology vehicle.

Shortly after joining General Motors, he arranged a meeting with vice president of GM vehicle design, Wayne Cherry. While the Cien certainly showed the world Cadillac was more than capable of designing and building a supercar to rival Ferrari and Lamborghini, Cadillac should also design and build a concept car that embraced the legend and legacy of Cadillac style and engineering as well. Lutz said he wanted to see a car that went beyond the V-12 in the Cien to a V-16 in this new concept car, enveloped in a sweeping body design on a very long wheelbase. The two men exchanged ideas, but Lutz made it clear what he would like to see.

Cherry agreed to get his designers working on it and he would have Lutz look at some preliminary sketches in several days to get a design direction.[6]

The designers at Cadillac's design studio worked several days on a number of designs, and Cherry called Lutz over to the vaunted luxury brand's impressive design studio to show him what they had come up with. The sketches reflected the new hard-edge design philosophy the division had embraced, Art & Science. Lutz wasted no time explaining his design philosophy to the designers for this car, but realized this was early. When Cherry said the car could probably be ready in time for the Geneva Motor Show in March 2003, Lutz challenged Cherry to have it ready for the Detroit Auto Show in January 2003 because the car should make its debut on American soil at its premier venue. That was just fifteen months away. To create a fully finished and running concept car with a never-before-built new V-16 engine in so short a time would be most challenging.

Chris Bolognino, a veteran of numerous GM concept car programs, was called in to discuss the logistics of engineering and supervising all

The Sixteen Concept was the bold idea of Robert Lutz to recapture the Cadillac brand's fame as a builder of V-16 automobiles. It combined stylistic elements of Cadillac's Art & Science philosophy with Lutz's vision of the ultimate Cadillac of the 21st Century (GM Media).

the facets of the concept car that would become known simply as the Sixteen. As with any new concept, the Sixteen had to reflect many new technologies that would or could make their way into production Cadillacs. Like the Cien, the Sixteen was designed from the ground up, with hardly an off-the-shelf part anywhere in the car. The V-16 engine would borrow certain engine geometry from the forthcoming 4th generation small-block V-8. The target output of the engine was to be an astounding 1000 horsepower. GM had the engineering resources to design this engine and the car's chassis and suspension in the virtual realm, thus saving precious time. Bolognino would also call in some of the best of GM specialist vendors both in America and in Europe to manufacture virtually everything that would go into the Sixteen.

While the Cadillac designers worked during the fall of 2001 on refining Lutz's vision for the Sixteen, work immediately began on the design of the engine, the driveline, and the platform it would power. From the very beginning, Lutz realized the car would be extremely heavy if aluminum was not used extensively throughout the car. Alcoa was called on to provide design and engineering assistance in the design of the Sixteen's body structure, suspension design and eventual production of the car's aluminum body panels. Alcoa worked concurrently with GM in providing the design and prototype components in the closing months of 2001 to show what the structure for the car would be. This would include a rigid structural backbone comprising a reinforced central tunnel with composite floor panels giving the needed stiffness and strength, suspension towers and control arms front and rear, as the Sixteen would be designed to employ four-wheel steering.[7]

In late December just before Christmas, Cherry again invited Lutz to the Cadillac design studio to look over the latest designs they had produced. Inside the classic design dome where so many production and concept car designs had been displayed over the decades, many renderings were mounted on easels for Lutz to review while the lead designer Brian Smith and his designers stood by proudly, others nervously. It did not go well. Lutz apparently didn't like anything he saw. The designers were incredulous. Lutz's vision of voluptuous design collided directly with the new design philosophy of Art & Science. Lutz later told *Newsweek* the designs he saw that day were "too angular or too bricklike or look like something out of 'Buck Rodgers [*sic*].'"[8] Somewhat exasperated, Lutz voiced his disagreement with the design direction of the Sixteen and again explained what he was really looking for. Cherry defended the edgy look of the designs presented, but promised Lutz they would make another attempt at what the father of the Dodge Viper was looking for in this Cadillac concept.

The centerpiece of the Sixteen was, indeed, the engine, and GM would bring to bear some of the most sophisticated tools in its computer capabilities to design the XV16—the first Cadillac V-16 in more than half a century. In the early months of 2002, design work began on this engine at GM's Powertrain High Performance Vehicle Group. Among the performance features to be incorporated were variable cam timing and Displacement on Demand. This engine would be an overhead valve design, not a DOHC like the Northstar. In fact, GM wanted to push the OHV technology and breathe new life into the venerable valvetrain design for a new generation of engines built by GM. The basis of the XV16's architecture was the Gen IV small-block V-8 about to be released in the Corvette. Another specialized group was brought in for the XV16—the GM Powertrain Synthesis and Analysis group in Pontiac, Michigan. An array of powerful engine design and analysis software was brought to bear on the huge engine, which would have a displacement of 827 cubic inches. In this specialized group, the individual engine parts were designed, analyzed for strength and durability, and any stress-risers detected and eliminated. Then the individual modeled parts were assembled into the engine, and other software could perform an operating engine with incoming air, injected fuel, combustion, and exhaust. Actual engine output in terms of horsepower and torque could also be calculated and determined with this software. It could even determine the degree of vibration created by the rotating and reciprocating parts in the engine model.

The purpose of such sophisticated software was to reduce the design time, lower the cost of part testing and development, and optimize the production part and eventual assembly. The cylinder block and cylinder heads were modeled and computational fluid dynamics employed to actually simulate the precise ratio of fuel and air molecules flowing through the engine. Even 87 octane gasoline (not recommended) could be specified to evaluate performance, and the engine coolant could be routed through the engine as well. Every component in the engine was designed and optimized in this way. The fully assembled computer model of the XV16 was started and put through the same development testing that would actually take place on an engine dynamometer. The revealed weak points were noted and changes made, overly robust parts were pared down to reduce weight, and redesigned parts assembled in the engine model and tested once again.

By the end of January 2002, Cherry called Lutz to say he felt they had nailed down the design concept he was seeking and to come by the studio for another look. This time, there were one-third-scale clay models of various designs. This is an important phase in any car design because it can be seen in the round, as opposed to a computer screen or a rendering. One design in particular caught Lutz's attention and they discussed its merits and possible improvements. Lutz wanted the roofline lower to make it more dramatic. The battle between Lutz's compound curves and Smith's hard edges continued. The design of the Sixteen would continue to evolve. By March 2002, a full-size clay model with a split representation of the more sharply defined design on one half of the model, and a more voluptuous interpretation on the other half, was displayed outside the design studio for the first time. This is a design technique that has been used by GM, and other manufacturers, for many years. As Smith expected, Lutz wanted a blending of the two design concepts. It was back to the drawing boards once again, but time was running out like sand through an hourglass.

At Alcoa, the company worked on the design of the car's structural backbone. It would not use the traditional unibody or spaceframe design.

The body design of the Sixteen with its 140-inch wheelbase took several months to evolve. Cadillac partnered with Alcoa Aluminum, and all the body panels and much of the car's structure were aluminum (GM Media).

The Sixteen would employ a new method Bolognino described as "endoskeletal construction." This was to be a careful assembly of formed aluminum and composite structural sandwich sheet with tubular extrusions welded to it to form the central structure or backbone. The front and rear bulkheads served as the shoulders and hips, metaphorically speaking, and these bulkheads were cast in one piece of aluminum. Other key aluminum components were visible, and these included the base windshield cowling and the 24-inch forged aluminum wheels that would carry the weight and power of the Sixteen.[9] However, before the effort could proceed, the car's design had to be finalized.

The first week in May, what was hoped to be the last design review took place once again at the design center with full-size clay models having a special surface film applied to give it the finished appearance of paint and glass. The operative word that had been bandied about for several months was "heritage." There was even a model from GM's London design studio. Finally, Smith's representation of the Sixteen got the nod, with some subtle changes Lutz requested. One design element that Lutz particularly liked was the classic butterfly hood, just like the V-16 Cadillacs of the 1930s. That was a functional feature of many other cars of the day, but had not been used on a contemporary car in many years. Now, Smith had just one month to finalize the design before handing it over to the other responsible parties so they could proceed with their tasks.

With the engine parts essentially finalized by the summer of 2002, the first aluminum castings were ordered from a specialist foundry in Germany known as Becker CAD CAM CAST. (An American office was eventually established in Detroit.) This company was able to make casting molds directly from the 3D computer models using a laser sintering process. The engine block took a full month while the cylinder heads took somewhat less time. With time very short, everyone had to work fast to make the aluminum engine parts in time for engine assembly with the January auto show looming.

The job of custom machining of the engine parts, assembly and testing of the XV16 engine was given to Katech, Inc., in Clinton Township, Michigan. Katech had a solid reputation in Detroit for building specialized engines for the city's auto manufacturers and for racing teams around the United States. The massive cylinder heads were machined using the CAD models and the ports were hand-ported due to their length; the cylinder heads could not fit in the company's five-axis CNC head porting machine.

Katech machined the V-16 cylinder block, while the line boring of the main bearing and camshaft bearing locations was performed by Schwartz Machine.[10]

Katech was also responsible for many other components, including the handsome valve covers, which took their design inspiration from the classic V-16, and the intake plenum and throttle bodies. The forged steel crankshaft was manufactured by Dearborn Crankshaft, again from the 3D CAD model. The camshafts were machined by LSM. As these parts were delivered to Katech, they were carefully inspected and checked. These parts were one-of-a-kind and anything out of tolerance had to be detected here, and not discovered after a catastrophic engine failure. The tube exhaust manifolds, another visual as well as functional element of the engine, were manufactured by another specialized supplier in Detroit. The XV16 underwent its own methodical program management at Katech. An October 2002 date was established for the first engine start of the XV16.

The XV16 in the tight engine bay of the Sixteen Concept. The butterfly opening hood was also a nod to the classic era. The spark plug wires and fuel injectors were cleverly concealed under the induction plenum (GM Media).

An essential design element of the engine was that there would be no visible ignition wires or fuel injectors and fuel rails to the injectors. The heads and intake plenum were designed to hide the injectors and ignition wiring so all that was visible from the top of the engine were the two chromed throttle bodies bolted to the inlet manifold with the polished and ribbed valve covers. Beneath the valve covers were the chromed tube exhaust manifolds bolted to the cylinder heads. The XV16 was to be a supreme visual statement from Cadillac, clearly visible with the fully opened butterfly hood. Wayne Cherry later stated, "The engine bay really pays tribute to the V-16. It's like a setting for a diamond, clean and simple. The under-hood was designed with the same care and attention as the interior."[11]

Finally, the assembled XV16 was ready for its first startup and test. October 30, 2002, was set for the engine start. The announcement went out to GM principals involved in the XV16 and the Sixteen Concept. Nat-

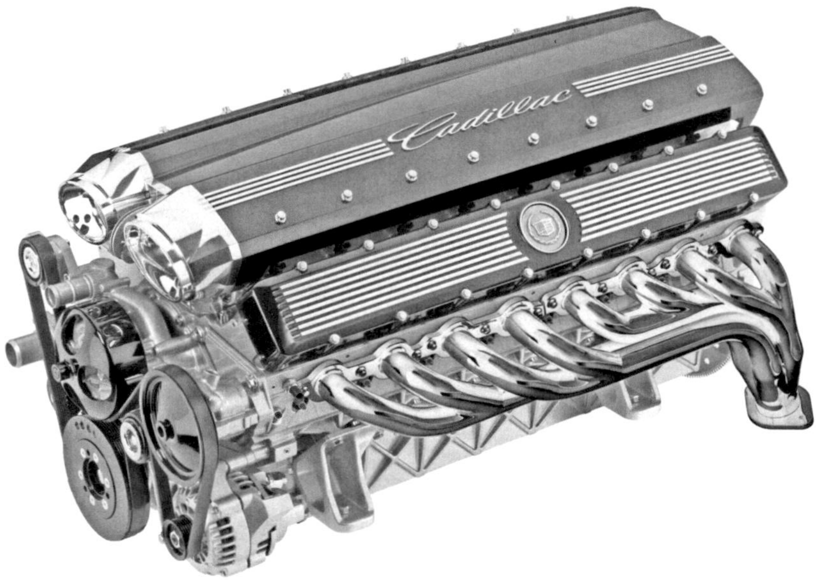

2003 XV16 Concept Engine

The XV16 was a quintessential industrial design statement that borrowed styling cues from Cadillac's original V-16 engine of the 1930s. The engine was capable of generating 1000 horsepower but also employed Displacement on Demand to improve fuel economy (GM Media).

urally, Katech technicians started and ran the engine on their dyno to verify everything was operating as it should and there were no surprises. GM's Tom Stephens, who was head of GM Powertrain, Wayne Cherry, and three dozen other engineers and personnel crowded into the Katech facility and close to the dyno cell windows to witness the startup of the mighty XV16. The superbly balanced V-16 was extremely smooth running after the start, but the surprise came shortly later. The Katech technician slowly increased the throttle. As the digital readouts spooled up past 700 horsepower, the barely muffled exhaust could be felt as well as heard. Then came 800 horsepower, a cheer at 900 horsepower, and when the readout read 1000 horsepower there was applause. The engine produced 980 lb.-ft. of torque at 3,600 rpm.

With the Sixteen Concept far from complete, real-world calibration had to be performed on the engine. To achieve that end, a GMC Yukon was taken to the GM Tech Center, where the engine compartment was modified to accept the big engine, and this test mule would be used to perform further tests. The only transmission in production to accept the torque of the XV16 was the 4L85-E used with GM's 8.2 liter big block V-8. The XV16 had to be tested in real-world conditions so the engineers could complete their calibration of the engine and finalize the software, confirm the performance of Displacement on Demand, and check the camshaft phasing operation, emissions, overall performance, and of course, the expected smoothness of the engine. The Yukon's throttle was limited to 45 percent of its total travel, and the test and calibration engineers marveled at the engine's effortless torque and capability to smoke the SUV's tires in the first three gears.

Lutz was anxious to test drive the mule, and in early December 2002, he was able to get behind the wheel of the Yukon with its truly one-of-a-kind V-16 engine. It was hard to believe the engine was capable of generating 1000 horsepower, but the throttle limiter would not allow Lutz to explore the engine's maximum output; neither he nor Cadillac could afford engine damage that would prevent the Sixteen from running under its own power. The snow on the ground of the GM Tech Center had been plowed from a suitable test area for Lutz. With his trademark cigar clenched between his teeth and smiling from ear to ear, he put the SUV through some rudimentary paces to see how the engine performed, fishtailing the vehicle repeatedly due to the engine's unprecedented torque. In exclamation, Lutz said, "Ah—the mighty 16!"[12]

The Sixteen program now shifted north of Detroit to Plymouth and a specialist car builder, Special Projects, where the Sixteen concept car was taking shape. On New Year's Eve, there were no champagne corks popping at Special Projects. The special Midnight Silver paint was being mixed in preparation for the twenty coats that would be applied. Installation of the interior, the engine and many of the car's other components would have to wait until the paint was applied and allowed to dry. Bolognino worried about whether the Sixteen could be completed in time for the Detroit Auto Show. Special Projects assured him it would be done and the car driven to verify all worked as planned, but no one would be getting much sleep. It was a 24-hour-a-day effort for the next several days.

Lutz piled on the misery by saying he wanted the Sixteen for a special unveiling at the redecorated Detroit Opera House and a one-million-dollar, one-night extravaganza to the automotive media and VIPs. With all the glitz that GM was capable of, the collected multitude heard the start of the Sixteen's engine from behind a curtain, which then parted. Bob Lutz was behind the wheel, and he slowly drove the car down a draped ramp to its display area and the incredulous expressions on all the faces. It was one of Lutz's greatest personal moments in an automotive career that spanned decades. As he stated a number of times over the next several days, the Cadillac Sixteen would prove to the world that GM's luxury division would take a back seat to no one. After the debut at the Detroit Opera House, the $3 million Sixteen was loaded into an enclosed transport and taken to the Detroit Auto Show venue and carefully moved to its reserved display area, where it would be shown to the world's automotive press.

The veil of secrecy surrounding the Sixteen had remained until the auto show with selected leaks to the press over the previous months about a super luxury concept in the works at Cadillac. The mystery was over as of the first press day of the show, before the general public could attend. Lutz was the point man for Sixteen before the press that first day.

"The Sixteen is a modern interpretation of everything that made Cadillac the standard of the world and can again," he told the automotive journalists as camera strobes flashed with the Sixteen slowly rotating on the turntable. "It's a reminder of a glorious past as well as a progressive statement. Cadillac's tradition is rich, but in the next several years it will be introducing vehicles as solid, dynamic and beautifully designed as anything it's ever done. And Sixteen is a harbinger of this new era."[13]

With the butterfly hood raised, the press could see the unprecedented

Tom Stephens, group vice president for GM Global Powertrain, announced the 13.6-liter XV16 engine at the 2003 Detroit Auto Show. The XV16 was conceived to show the performance capabilities of an overhead valve engine as a technology driver comparable to the DOHC XV12 (GM Media).

long XV16 also made a stunning industrial design statement. Thomas G. Stephens, GM group vice-president of GM Powertrain, also had key things to say about the powerful yet refined and even fuel-efficient XV16 engine. "The XV16 is an uncomplicated, technically elegant design that sets new levels for efficient, silky-smooth, ultra-quiet operation," Stevens stated. "Its power and torque levels are also beyond any other engine of which we know."[14]

Perhaps no one but Robert Lutz had the audacity to conceive and champion such an overwhelming concept car as the Cadillac Sixteen. It stemmed from his unshakable belief that Cadillac had to regain its once pre-eminent position among American luxury cars it held during the classic era of the 1930s. However, he also knew the concept project would stretch GM's technological capabilities and thus provide a corporate-wide benefit, while adding prestige to the Cadillac division. And to prove the Sixteen was not a turntable show car, Lutz made sure the editors of the key automotive magazines could literally get their hands on the car and, yes, drive it.

An editor from *Motor Trend* was given permission to drive the Sixteen around the GM Proving Ground in Milford, Michigan, in the summer of 2003. The editor had to remind himself the car had virtually no acoustic insulation in the engine compartment or elsewhere in the car, and the engine exhibited the characteristic exhaust chugging sound from its steel tube headers. That gave the Sixteen something of a coarse sound while the editor sat behind the wheel, but the interior was certainly luxurious and comfortable enough. Despite the car's massive size, it moved quickly and precisely, and the car's handling displayed no roll with light steering input. The editor accelerated quickly, impressed with its abundant torque, then quickly let off the gas pedal to sense any protest from the transmission, but the deceleration was turbine smooth. The editor was less impressed with the car's braking ability, but this was no fully-developed production car. The Sixteen's low-speed active four-wheel steering helped reduce the turning circle. Less than an hour behind the wheel of the Sixteen convinced the editor the car was the most refined concept car he had ever driven.

The Cadillac Sixteen, like many of GM's priceless concept cars, has been ensconced in GM's Heritage Center since it made the rounds of the auto show circuit and select driving opportunities for magazine editors. For the Amelia Island Concours d'Elegance in March 2013, the Sixteen came with ten other Cadillac concept cars dating back to 1949. Cadillac has always had some of the most provocative concept cars ever built by General Motors. It is always a tantalizing prospect to imagine driving a mid-engine V-12 Cien or a V-16 Sixteen. In a practical sense, these concept cars achieve all they are designed to do, and they are the best of their kind in the world.

6

Cadillac Goes Racing with the Northstar V-8

Cadillac has a postwar racing history stretching back to 1950 and the 24 Hours of Le Mans. For the 1950 running of the race, independent racer Briggs Cunningham chose Cadillac to compete. He used two cars. The first was a two-door Coupe de Ville, which was race prepared by Frick-Tappett Motors, to compete in one class. It had a curious black and white color scheme with a visible "3" painted on the front of the hood and flanks of the car. The second car was something of an unlimited model in that the body was removed and engineers and aerodynamicists at Grumman Aircraft designed a body that reduced drag. It had no roof and a minimal windscreen. At the Le Mans track, the French quickly dubbed this second car "Le Monstre."

Two of the drivers on Cunningham's team, Sam and Miles Collier, had driven at Le Mans before, and they would drive the Coupe de Ville. Briggs Cunningham chose to drive the experimental Cadillac. The Cadillac V-8s withstood the grueling 24-hour endurance race, but Cunningham had the indignity of sliding off the course at one point into a protective sand bank; he was forced to dig his car out, which cost him precious time. The Coupe de Ville finished an impressive 10th overall against very worthy and more heavily financed teams, while Cunningham and his co-driver Phil Walters in the "monster" finished right behind, in 11th.[1]

Team Cunningham liked the rock-solid Cadillac V-8, and Briggs had the idea to stuff that engine into a much smaller car, the Healey Silverstone. Frick-Tappett Motors built a testbed vehicle and Cunningham competed with it at a Palm Beach Shores competition, winning second place. He went on to the Watkins Glen Grand Prix and won first and then second in two separate events in the fall of 1951. These were a prelude to that year's 24 Hours of Le Mans. However, Cadillac had second thoughts about supplying engines to Cunningham's team, and the division said they would not support him anymore. The reasons for this are vague, though perhaps Cadillac felt racing was not the image it wanted for its luxury cars. Cunningham's second choice for motive power was the Chrysler Firepower Hemi V-8. This turned out to be a very good choice. The cars built had the first "C" designations, and this series of cars would compete successfully over the next several years.

In the United States, Cadillac was not the GM brand of choice of stock car racers. That fell to Chevrolet and Pontiac, and to a lesser extent, Oldsmobile. The relationship of the GM divisions in support of racing fluctuated from official support to clandestine support and back again. This had a lot to do with who was head of GM and who was managing each division. Cadillac was never again officially involved in racing until the corporation launched GM Motorsports in the 1990s and Cadillac was eventually brought into the fold.

The Indy Racing League Aurora V-8

During the late 1990s, GM and its Motorsports division became actively involved in long-duration road racing events like the 24 Hours of Daytona and the 12 Hours of Sebring. The engine of choice for this racing was based on the DOHC 48-valve Northstar V-8 with a 4.0 liter displacement. In 1995 and 1996 this engine helped achieve overall wins at the 24 Hours of Daytona and the 12 Hours of Sebring.

Every racing series in America and Europe has its own set of rules governing everything from engine displacement and configuration to racing vehicle design and other requirements. In January 1996, Oldsmobile general manager John Rock announced plans to design and develop a naturally aspirated racing version of its Aurora V-8 to compete in the Indy Racing League (IRL) series. This actually involved more than just the engine, including the racing car itself. Oldsmobile partnered with the racing engine builders Katech, in Mt. Clemens, Michigan, in the development of this 4.0 liter racing engine. GM Motorsports was also involved, having a vested interest in the success of this program. Ed Keating was the GM Motorsports IRL program manager and chief engineer of the Aurora IRL V-8. The Aurora IRL V-8 was based of the 4.0 liter 32-valve DOHC variant of the Cadillac Northstar V-8. While many of the dimensions and geometry were shared by the production and racing Aurora 4.0 V-8s, that was where similarities ended.

GM Motorsports spent most of 1996 doing the design engineering and limited production planning for the Aurora IRL V-8 engine block, lower case, cylinder heads, induction manifolds and other parts. The validated parts were delivered to Katech in the summer of 1996. Katech technicians performed the requisite blueprinting as the first engine was carefully assembled. On September 20, 1996, the engine was started up on the Katech dynamometer with engineers from GM Motorsports and Oldsmobile present. Under a very carefully prescribed testing sequence, the engine was brought up through a series of performance levels and engine speeds.

"It was very gratifying to see the Indy Aurora V-8 run for the first time," Keating was quoted as saying in a subsequent press release. "But, as soon as the engine fired up, we were already thinking about the next step. It was a relief when the engine started right up, but we weren't able to stop and celebrate the event. Everyone associated with this program is working under very tight deadlines, and there is still a great deal of work to be done both on the dyno and on the race track. If everything goes as planned, we'll complete the inspection, reassemble the engine, and have it back running on the dyno again in a few days. The initial tests were very encouraging, but they are only the first step in a continuous process of testing and development."[2]

Keating and his team at GM Motorsports had only three months to complete development testing of the engine and racing cars. Also, racing drivers and teams had to get their hands on the cars to get familiar with the performance of the engine and car on the track in time for the first race of the 1997 Indy Racing League season. That race was scheduled for January 25, 1997, at the Walt Disney World Speedway (WDWS) in Bay Lake, Florida. The WDWS is a one-mile short track with three straights and three turns. This first race of the IRL season was a 200-mile event. Tony Stewart in his IRL Aurora V-8–powered car won the pole position for the race. The teams running this engine dominated the race, which was ultimately called on the 149th lap due to heavy rain.

GM Motorsports IRL Aurora V-8 also won the next IRL race, the 200-mile event at Phoenix International Raceway in Avondale, Arizona, on March 23, 1997. At the runup to the IRL Indy 500, on May 10, driver Arie Luyendyk qualified for the pole position in his Treadway Racing's

IRL Aurora V-8–powered Indy car with an average speed of 218.263 mph. Five days later, this engine won the Louis Schwitzer Award for excellence and innovation in racing engine and car design, presented by the Indianapolis Chapter of the Society of Automotive Engineers (SAE).

"We feel honored that the Indy Aurora V-8 was chosen for this prestigious award," Keating said in receiving the award on behalf of GM Motorsports and Oldsmobile. "It has taken a tremendous effort by everyone involved in the program, including our development partners, component suppliers, engine builders, and racing teams to produce the Indy Aurora V-8 in volume while working under the constraints of a tight deadline and a price target."[3]

The Le Mans Prototype (LMP)

In the Indy Racing League (IRL), this IRL Aurora V-8 won every IRL event including two Indianapolis 500 races. This engine served as the basis for what would become known as the Cadillac Le Mans Prototype, or LMP for short. Jeff Kettman was the Cadillac Northstar LMP program manager. The winning chassis running that engine was the Mk III designed and built by Riley & Scott. When plans came together to select a chassis to be powered by a 4.0-liter Northstar, this chassis was the obvious choice. The Mk III was a carbon fiber monocoque design with aluminum honeycomb core that was very light and extremely strong.[4] This ensured a stable and predictable racecar performance as well as driver safety. Riley & Scott had sophisticated chassis fabrication equipment at the manufacturing facility, and each Mk III chassis could be manufactured with consistency.

With the known design and qualities of the Mk III, the body would have to be new, and GM drew on its Computer Fluid Dynamics software to design it. CFD allows the design of the body while permitting evaluation of drag, inlet flow, and other aerodynamic parameters. A forty percent rolling scale model was first used for extensive wind tunnel testing to get real-world data on drag and downforce. A full-size body was then fabricated for actual wind tunnel testing to refine features of the body and gain actual numbers with respect to drag and downforce. The engine would be a new twin turbocharged design, so intercooler inlet locations on the top of the body needed to be determined and optimized for best performance.

The new racecar suspension drew from existing Mk III design having unequal length wishbones and pushrod-activated integral shock absorber and spring at each location. The specific geometry was tuned to this specific car and power application. The LMP featured rack and pinion power steering, necessary because of the large caster angles and very high downforce at speed. Special Cadillac LMP wheels were manufactured by BBS; rear wheels measured 14.5 inches wide by 18 inches in diameter, while the front measured 13.0 inches wide by 18 inches in diameter. Brakes were race-proven from the original MK III chassis.[5]

Dave Spitzer was the engine program manager for the Cadillac Northstar LMP when the program was launched in 1999. It was planned from the beginning that the racing Northstar V-8 would be fitted with twin IHI turbochargers. To ensure durability of the engine as well as superior power, Spitzer called on McLaren Performance Technologies, Inc. (MPT) in Livonia, Michigan. Spitzer met with MPT president Wiley R. McCoy to work out the engine development program. The goal was to get just under 600 horsepower from the 4.0 liter Northstar V-8. GM Motorsports and MPT collaborated on the design development of this engine, with MPT responsible for the engine assembly and performance

The twin turbocharged Northstar V-8 was purpose-built for racing to power the LMP001 for racing competitions in Europe and the United States (GM Media).

and validation testing. Coupled to the mighty longitudinally oriented LMP Northstar V-8 was an Emco six-speed transmission.[6]

Development of the engine and the racecar proceeded smoothly to the point the first two cars began track testing in the summer of 1999. The finished cars both weighed just under 2,000 pounds. Two separate teams would race in North America and in Europe. Racing efforts would be focused on the American Le Mans Series with Team Cadillac. Driot Arnoux Motor Sport (DAMS) from France, sponsored by Motorola, would race the car in the European Sports Racing World Cup. However, each team did participate in some of the other racing series competitions. Each team received two cars, all built by Riley & Scott. Each car had a specific alphanumeric designation. LMP-00–001 was a test vehicle and never raced. LMP-00–002, LMP-00–005 and LMP-00–006 went to French team. LMP-00–003 and LMP-00–004 were raced by Team Cadillac for the 2000 racing season.

Team Cadillac Efforts in 2000

LMP-00–003 and LMP-00–004 ran qualifying races in January 2000 for the 24 Hours of Daytona in February. The cars placed 6th and 12th respectively. LMP-00–003 (car number 5) was 5th on the starting grid and LMP-00–004 (car number 6) was 8th on the starting grid at the start of the race on February 6. The number 5 car finished 14th overall and the number 6 car finished 13th overall out of a starting grid of 79 cars. This was an impressive start for a new car and engine design against seasoned cars and drivers.

The next key race in the American series was the 12 Hours of Sebring on March 18. LMP-00–003 (car number 19) placed 6th. LMP-00–004 (car number 9) placed a distant 35th. Interestingly, Cadillac decided to have these two cars also compete in the 24 Hours of Le Mans along with the two French DAMS cars. All four cars competed in the April 30 qualifying races. Team Cadillac took as a positive sign their cars were numbered 1 (LMP-00–003) and 2 (LMP-00–004) for the legendary endurance race. In the April qualifying race, No. 1 placed 16th overall and the No. 2 car placed 14th. In the 24-hour race that began on June 18, the No. 1 car finished 21st overall and the No. 2 car finished 22nd. The French team car No. 3 finished the race 19th overall, but the No. 4 car did not finish (DNF). Nevertheless, this was an impressive showing for Cadillac's first appearance at Le Mans in decades.

The Cadillac Le Mans Prototype LMP-01 first competed in the year 2000. It employed a proven racing chassis and a twin-turbocharged Northstar V-8 (GM Media).

"As certain ancillary aspects of the car suffered failure [clutch and gearbox], the Northstar engine performed up to Cadillac's ultra-high standards," said Jeff Kettman. "Sure, everyone here is disappointed that we didn't finish higher, but we are extremely pleased with the durability of this engine."[7]

Team Cadillac's LMP-00–004 car was entered in the September 10 race at Portland International Raceway. The car finished 8th in a starting field of 25 cars. On the 30th of that month, both LMP-00–003 and LMP-00–004 were entered in the Petit Le Mans competition at Road Atlanta Motorsports Center. This was a 1,000-mile race. Neither car finished in the top three finishers. LMP-00–003 finished 8th and the team car finished 7th. The last race of the 2000 season for Team Cadillac was at Laguna Seca, California, held on October 15. This was also a two hour and forty-five minute race. The LMP-00–004 car competed and placed 7th.[8]

Motorola DAMS in 2000

The French racing team of DAMS raced LMP-00–002 and LMP-00–005 for most of the 2000 racing season. Before competing in the Barcelona race on March 26, the team got familiar racing their two cars in the 12 Hours of Sebring along with Team Cadillac on March 18. The French team did not do well in their first racing with the twin-turbo Northstar V-8. The No. 31 car (-005) placed a dismal 27th, while the No. 32 car (-002) did not finish the race at all. However, they did gain valuable experience in sorting the cars out, which were prepped for the Barcelona race by Riley & Scott and flown to Spain.

The Barcelona race was not an endurance event, being only two and a half hours in duration. In the race -005 was No. 11 and finished 8th, and -002 was No. 12 and finished 7th. The following month the team went to Monza, Italy, for the 500 km competition. The -002 car finished an impressive 4th, but this would the highest ranking finish for the Cadillacs in the 2000 European season. The -005 car did not finish the race due to mechanical problems.

Two weeks later, the French team was in their home country for the 24 Hours of Le Mans. In the qualifying races on April 30, the No. 3 -005 car finished 11th and the No. 4 -002 car finished 12th. Then the team was off to the iconic Silverstone race track in England for the 500 km race on

Separate American and French teams raced the LMP in 2000. The entire French DAMS racing team with two of the LMPs pose near the stands before the 2000 24 Hours of Le Mans (GM Media).

May 13. It was nearly a replay of the Monza race. The -002 car did not finish the race and the -005 car finished 5th. The following week the team traveled to Belgium for the competition at Spa. This proved the most disappointing showing of the entire 2000 season. Neither car finished the race, despite the fact it was only a two-and-a-half-hour competition.

The DAMS team did not have time to complain because the Le Mans race was coming up in June. This race is famous for running all the different automobile classes during the same 24-hour event. Virtually stock production Porsches share the track with the most powerful of Ferraris, but this is not a race so much of speed as of endurance. All four Cadillac LMPs were on the starting grid on June 18. The Audi R8 dominated the race. At the end of 24 hours, the Cadillac LMP-00–005 finished 19th overall, the best of the four cars entered.

After Le Mans, the most grueling race in Europe is perhaps the 1000 km Nürburgring in Germany. The race took place on July 9. Considering the formidable and experienced teams and cars entered, the DAMS Cadillacs did well. The damaged -002 car was replaced with LMP-00–006; this car finished the race in 5th place. The -005 car finished 16th. Both Team Cadillac and DAMS competed in the Petit Le Mans at Road Atlanta Motorsports Center on September 30. The French team finished 6th and 13th. In their last race of the season, DAMS traveled down under to compete in the Adelaide, Australia, race on December 31. After 1000 km, the team finished 19th and 20th. Both Team Cadillac and DAMS would be back in 2001 after applying all the lessons learned and trying to make the cars as reliable as possible.

The 2001 Racing Season

During the winter months of 2001, GM Racing worked to improve the Cadillac LMP. Extensive changes were made to the chassis and Northstar engine. Changes to the engine included a new 180-degree crankshaft, and more than 100 other mechanical improvements or refinements, including engine control electronics. The engine was lowered an additional inch in the chassis, subtly improving the car's center of gravity. Chassis improvements included a new bellhousing and gearbox which helped to stiffen the chassis. The suspension received upgrades with new uprights, wishbones and hubs, and the car also received a new power steering system. Even the racing tires were new, as Team Cadillac switched to racing Michelins.

The improved LMP was taken to the Carolina Motorsports Park racetrack in Kershaw, South Carolina, at the end of March to undergo extensive testing to sort out the improvements and get team drivers Wayne Taylor and Max Angelelli familiar with the car's performance and handling characteristics. Two LMPs were evaluated for Team Cadillac and DAMS in preparation for the 2001 racing season. The first race for Cadillac to compete in was also the biggest: the 24 Hours of Le Mans on June 16 and 17.[9] Team Cadillac did not enter this race, preferring to focus on American competitions, so the gauntlet was carried by the DAMS team. They drove two cars, the LMP-00–004 and the LMP-00–007. The team of Taylor, Angelelli and Tinseau rotated their driving stints during the 24-hour race. The car held up well and finished 15th overall. Drivers Bernard, Collard and Coossens did not fare as well; their -007 did not finish the race.

The -004 car was then returned to the United States and would compete with the LMP-00–006 car for the rest of the season. In July at Sears

The French DAMS driving team pose with LMP001 No. 6 in the pits at Le Mans prior to the 2001 race (GM Media).

The paint scheme for the LMP was changed for the 2001 racing season. Here the DAMS No. 5 car is shown during a competition (GM Media).

Point, a two hour and 45 minute race, Team Cadillac finished 12th and 24th. They had better luck at Mosport on August 19, with the -006 car finishing third, and -004 car finishing fourth. The team immediately left for the Mid-Ohio race to be held August 25. There, Team Cadillac finished seventh and eighth. Then it was on to the iconic Laguna Seca race in September. Once again the drivers of the two cars drove like a tag team, and finished fourth and fifth overall. The last race of the season was the Petit Le Mans in October. The -004 car with the team of Angelelli, Tinseau and Taylor finished fourth and the -006 car with drivers Goossens and Collard finished right behind in fifth, closing out the 2001 season.[10]

The New LMP-02

During the 2001 racing season, GM Racing had been working on a completely new LMP for Team Cadillac to compete with in 2002 and 2003. Cadillac would celebrate its centennial birthday in 2002, and their premier race car needed to reflect the design engineering to compete and beat the competition. The second generation car would be practically new from the ground up. It was designed and built by a completely new team.

"In the first year of the program," Jeff Kettman stated, "we learned about the level of competition we faced. In the second year, we focused on collecting data and accumulating experience while racing a highly modified LMP 01 chassis. Now in the third year of the program, we are introducing the new Cadillac Northstar LMP 02—a car that incorporates the lessons we have learned and embodies the knowledge we have gained."[11]

The basic tenet of racing car development is continuous improvement of the engine, transmission, chassis and body. All of this happened with the LMP 02. The twin-turbocharged Northstar V-8 had proved its durability, reliability and power generation, but there were still other areas where performance could be enhanced. This engine was conceived and developed to compete in and qualify for several different racing competitions in America and Europe. The 180-degree crankshaft introduced for 2001 was based on a design developed for the Indy Racing League (IRL). In addition, the LMP Northstar V-8 had ties to the naturally aspirated 4.0 liter engine used by GM's Opel division in the German Touring Car Masters (DTM) road racing series.

"This year (2002) we are incorporating cylinder head and valvetrain developments from the Opel DTM program that suit the operating range of the Northstar LMP engine," Jeff Keating explained at the time the new

The LMP-02 for 2002 was a completely new car, with performance enhancements to the twin-turbo Northstar V-8 (GM Media).

car was announced. "We are also pursuing improved performance and fuel efficiency through friction reduction, induction system tuning, and refinements in engine calibration and enhancements in oil scavenging to minimize parasitic windage losses."[12]

Coupled with the engine improvements was a new Xtrac six-speed transmission with pneumatically actuated paddle shifters mounted on the steering wheel. The pneumatic system was designed to operate independently of the engine's other systems to avoid dependence on engine oil pressure hydraulics. At its new level of development, the LMP 02 Northstar V-8 was developing over 600 horsepower.

To make improvements in the chassis and body for the LMP 02, GM Racing employed the latest technology tools available to it. This included computer-aided design and manufacturing (CAD/CAM), computational fluid dynamics (CFD), finite element analysis (FEA) and 3D computer solid modeling. GM Racing marshaled considerable resources in designing a new carbon fiber monocoque chassis under the design direction of Nigel Stroud. The change to a shorter wheelbase improved the aerodynamics and made the new car less sensitive to pitch.

Advances were achieved in construction of the monocoque chassis in how the halves were bonded together. Improvements were made in the side-mounted radiators for both engine and transmission cooling. Design changes in the driver cockpit also made it structurally safer. The double wishbone suspension now used F1-style cast stainless steel uprights that mounted the six-piston brake calipers and carbon fiber disc brake rotors. The LMP 02 had an overall length of 193 inches, a width of 78.75 inches, a height of just over 40.1 inches, and weighed 1984 pounds.

"Very seldom in racing can you talk about a program in its third year and say that you have an all-new race car, but that is exactly the case with the Cadillac LMP 02," said Herb Fishel, executive director of GM Racing said in a press release. He added, "[W]e are optimistic that the 2002 Cadillac LMP will be a credible contender in this fiercely competitive arena."[13]

The LMP 02 during 2002

GM chose to field just one team to race the LMP in 2002 and that was Team Cadillac; the DAMS drivers were off to other racing teams. Three LMP 02s were raced this season. At the 12 Hours of Sebring on March

Team Cadillac from the United States posing with cars No. 6 and No. 7 after passing technical inspection for the 2002 24 Hours of Le Mans. The No. 6 car finished 9th overall and the No. 7 car finished in 12th position in the grueling race (GM Media).

16, the team did poorly. The two cars entered finished 27th and 31st. At the qualifying races for Le Mans in May, the two cars finished 16th and 17th. At the premier racing event the following month, both cars finished the grueling race with an acceptable 9th and 12th overall. In the Grand Prix of Washington, D.C., on July 21, two LMP 02s placed 4th and a disappointing 29th (a DNF). In August at Mosport, the two cars finished 3rd and 6th. The following month at Laguna Seca, the LMP 02–002 finished in the money in 3rd, but the team LMP 02–003 finished back in the field in 28th place. In October in Miami the -002 car finished in 2nd, its best showing of the season, and the -003 car finished in 7th. At the Petit Le Mans, the last race of the season, the two cars finished 3rd and 4th.[14]

In its three years of racing, the Cadillac LMP with twin-turbocharged Northstar V-8 never won a single race. Nevertheless, these were impressive showings from Cadillac, which had not been a serious racing contender in decades. General Motors chose to back the racing efforts of its "halo" car, the Corvette. Today, Cadillac continues to race as part of boosting its brand image.

7

The Northstar V-8 in Other GM Cars

The Cadillac Northstar V-8 was indeed General Motors' premium V-8 engine for its luxury brand. It remained so until GM and Oldsmobile management wanted to improve the rather stodgy image of the Oldsmobile division. The first step in adding panache to Oldsmobile was to design and build a concept racecar called the Aerotech. And aero it definitely was. The Aerotech was designed to break speed records. In 1984, Oldsmobile was completing development of its dual overhead camshaft four valve-per-cylinder 2.3 liter inline four-cylinder engine it called the Quad 4.

To promote the technology of this Oldsmobile-engineered engine, the division conceived the Aerotech research vehicle. The sleek body was designed under the direction of Ed Welburn, the division's assistant chief designer. This was during the days at General Motors when each division did its own engineering and automobile styling. The Quad 4 was given to Batten Heads in Detroit, which extensively modified the engine with turbocharging to boost horsepower to between 800 and 900 horsepower. Oldsmobile hired legendary race driver A.J. Foyt to drive the car at the 7.7-mile Fort Stockton, Texas, oval test track. On August 27, 1987, Foyt got behind the wheel of the Aerotech and broke numerous records. It had a documented two-way average speed of 267.4 mph and on one leg of the track achieved 278.357 mph.

In the early 1990s, General Motors wanted to further improve Oldsmobile's image and market perception by conceiving a new model with the name Aurora and a new V-8 engine to power it. Cadillac was, at the time, engineering the Northstar DOHC V-8 with 4.6 liter displacement. Oldsmobile conceived a smaller displacement DOHC engine having 4.0 liters. To establish its engineering of this engine, the division chose to revisit the Aerotech and power it with its 4.0 DOHC Aurora V-8. However, in this record attempt, the engine would be basically stock, with the only change being different camshafts to boost horsepower; there was no turbocharging. The 1992 version of the Aerotech had the addition of driving lights and a few other refinements. Oldsmobile did not want to go for just top speed, but also endurance records this time out.

A small team of drivers returned with the Aurora V-8 Aerotech to the Fort Stockton test track in December 1992. The team of drivers drove the car 24 hours a day for eight days and broke 47 international records. The included the F.I.A. World Land Speed Record for 10,000 kilometers at 170.761 mph and the 25,000 kilometers at 158.386 mph. It also broke eighteen USAC National Land Speed records with a best of 181.988 mph, among numerous other national records.[1]

Oldsmobile used these new records to great success at the 1993 Detroit Auto Show, where the division announced it would introduce a new luxury model, the Aurora. It would have a distinct identity, having no Oldsmobile identity badging anywhere on its exterior. While the car was still in production development at the time, the timing was right to begin to build interest in the new car. It was drastically needed. Oldsmobile sales had been declining ever since the 1980s; the brand needed rejuvenating. After all, Oldsmobile had introduced one of the most successful automotive advertising campaigns with the "Rocket 88." Also, the front-wheel-drive Toronado for 1966 looked like a concept car that went into production. Oldsmobile had also introduced its own muscle car in 1964, the 4–4-2 (for 4-barrel carburetor, 4-speed manual transmission, and dual exhaust). By the late 1960s, Oldsmobile was doing very well in a crowded American market. This peaked in the 1970s and began a gradual sales decline during the 1980s as the average age of the Oldsmobile owner began climbing.

The 1995–1999 Aurora

The Oldsmobile Aurora went into production in January 1994 as a 1995 model. The Aurora's styling was completely different from any other GM automobile and it was undeniably handsome. It was designed and engineered to be structurally very strong for crash protection and to ensure a good ride in a smooth-handling car that was also quiet. It had standard leather seating surfaces, dual-zone climate control, a six-speaker sound system, power seats and windows, and luxurious burl walnut trim on the dash and door panels. Of course, the big news for mechanically minded buyers of the Aurora was the 4.0 liter DOHC 32-valve V-8. The engine was rated at 250 horsepower at 5600 rpm with 260 lb.-ft. of torque at 4400 rpm. The 4.0 liter engine had the same 3.3-inch stroke as the 4.6 L Northstar V-8, but a smaller 3.4-inch bore. To reduce engine weight, the intake manifold was made of glass-filled thermoplastic. The Aurora had a base list price of $31,370. Over 45,000 Auroras were sold in its first year of production.

Motor Trend magazine chose to put the Aurora head-to-head in a comparison test with the Mercedes-Benz C280 and the Lexus GS 300 in the September 1994 issue. The Aurora did impressively well against the formidable competition. In the words of one editor, "The Oldsmobile Aurora is the best car to roll out of General Motors in recent memory."[2] In the February 1995 issue, the editors then put the Aurora up against the Mazda Millenia and the BMW 530i. Although the Aurora had 40 more

The Oldsmobile Aurora was introduced for the 1995 model year and was powered by a 4.0 liter variant of the 4.6 liter Northstar V-8. The car made its debut at the Detroit Auto Show (GM Media).

The L47 DOHC 32-valve 4.0 liter V-8 in the Aurora was rated at 250 horsepower and had 260 lb.-ft. of torque. This engine was the basis of the racing version used by Cadillac for the LM1 racecar (GM Media).

horsepower than the Millenia, it was also significantly heavier. While fractionally faster to 60 mph than the BMW, it was slower than the Mazda. However, Oldsmobile still had the impressive durability records of the basically stock 32-valve DOHC Aurora V-8 Aerotech record run to point to in its marketing.

Motor Trend was sufficiently impressed with the Aurora to undertake a long-term test of the car to see "if the Aurora could go the distance." Aside from evaluating the car over a period of months, the editors also polled Aurora owners on a number of the car's features and performance in order to give readers a real-world response to it. Over 90 percent of the owners said the Aurora's handsome looks were a significant factor in the purchase decision. Owners felt the Aurora had a near-perfect balance of luxury ride and impressive handling. *Motor Trend* editors reported the Aurora achieved a speed of 63.6 mph through its slalom course, which virtually matched the automotive competition from Germany. On the skid-pad, the Aurora achieved 0.81 g. It could stop from 60 mph in 122 feet. The most annoying trait of the car to the editors was the optimistic fuel gauge. When the gauge read a quarter of a tank, in fact the Aurora was nearly out of gas. The magazine reported the Aurora achieved 17 mph in city driving and 24 mpg on the highway.[3]

For the next five production years, Oldsmobile did not alter the car or its engine in any significant way; it did not need to. The Aurora arrived on the market for 1995 fully developed, and it had one of the best maintenance records of any domestic automobile. Although unchanged, the car continued to draw admiring glances and acceptable sales for Oldsmobile. Most significant was that Aurora buyers traded in the four-year-old cars to buy a new one, and many households bought a second Aurora.

The Second Generation Aurora: Engine Improvements and a Shorter Car

After five years of production, the Aurora needed refreshing. Oldsmobile's engineers went through the engine to improve emissions, and to make it even quieter and slightly more fuel efficient. The four-valve combustion chamber was redesigned and employed new pistons and a new reaction-heated catalyst system introduced to lower emissions. Other improvements were made to the valvetrain to lower friction. Oldsmobile left the power output of the 4.0 liter engine at 250 horsepower at 5600 rpm. Surveys of Aurora owners reported the existing performance of the engine was more than adequate for the majority of the drivers, and Oldsmobile wanted to improve the car's mileage. This was achieved by shortening the car by half a foot and introducing lighter-weight materials throughout the vehicle.

The design aesthetic of the first-generation Aurora won praise from owners and the automotive press alike. However, it was too much to expect that a five-year-old design would remain untouched. For 2001, Aurora was subtly redesigned, and to some the car lost its distinctive looks. Nevertheless, the editors at *Motor Trend* liked the second-generation Aurora, which it tested for the April 2000 issue. In summary, the editors wrote: "This fresh Aurora is a fun-to-drive, remarkably well-executed, sporty sedan that nicely balances the luxury-comfort and responsive-agile sides of the driving equation at a reasonable price."[4]

The second-generation Aurora featured a less-than-successful body redesign that lost some of the original distinctive design (GM Media).

Oldsmobile management decided that 2003 would be the last production year for the Aurora, as sales of the car had not met expectations and the division was being shut down the following year. Still, for its last year, a forged steel crankshaft was introduced to improve the engine's noise, vibration and harshness (NVH) qualities. This made the engine even quieter and practically indestructible. The pistons received a Grafal polymer coating. Oldsmobile offered a limited-edition Aurora V-8 Collector Edition built in 500 units. The last 500 cars for 2003 received distinctive wheels, interior and exterior ornamentation, and a certificate with the owner's manual.

Aurora collectors who have performed classic performance-enhancing modifications to the 4.0 liter V-8 have boosted horsepower to almost 300. These include improved induction systems, changes to the engine microprocessor, and a less restrictive dual exhaust system.

The Rare Northstar V-8 Pontiac Bonneville GXP and Buick Lucerne

General Motors wanted to spread the Northstar V-8's wealth of technical engineering and operation to two of its other divisions, Pontiac and

Buick. Pontiac would be the first beneficiary. The Bonneville had always been Pontiac's more sporting sedan, so the division created a new model to showcase the 32-valve DOHC V-8: the Bonneville GXP. Introduced in 2004, the GXP featured fully independent performance-tuned suspension, an electronically controlled transaxle, and a 3.71 final drive ratio. It had an anti-lock braking system with larger front rotors and the GXP suspension was Cadillac's StabiliTrak. This car had a unique exhaust system from the Cadillac and had an impressive exhaust sound under hard acceleration. The Northstar V-8 itself remained unchanged at 275 horsepower.

Few automotive magazines showed interest in testing the Pontiac GXP. One of them was *Car & Driver*, which had a comparison test of V-8 sedans for its September 2004 issue. The editors had nothing to say about the use of the Northstar V-8 in the GXP until the end of the article. The editors harped on the garish and nonintuitive dashboard controls and instrumentation and the confusing mix of interior materials. The car's suspension over the handling course got mixed reviews. Despite the Bonneville's weight, the GXP still managed to get to 60 mph in 6.9 seconds.

When production of the Aurora ceased with the 2003 model year and the end of the Oldsmobile brand in 2004, GM ordered the top-of-the-line Pontiac Bonneville to get the Northstar V-8 for the 2004 model year. This was offered in the GXP option on the Bonneville (GM Media).

The Northstar V-8 installed in the 2004 Bonneville GXP featured the same specifications as the engine in FWD Cadillacs, but featured a brand-specific engine cover. Note the Pontiac emblem in the center of the cover (GM Media).

Amazingly, the Pontiac Bonneville GXP had a base list price just under $36,000. The editors felt the Chrysler 300C with its Hemi engine was a far better car in practically all respects and cost $4000 less.[5] Like the Oldsmobile division, Pontiac would later be closed down as part of GM's bankruptcy restructuring. The last production year would be 2009. The final production year for the Bonneville GXP was 2005.

Buick introduced the Lucerne model for 2006. This became the top-of-the-line model, replacing the Park Avenue and LeSabre—model names that had been in the Buick lineup for decades. The Lucerne came standard with GM's 3.8 liter V-6. Certainly for the majority of Buick buyers and the rental car market, this was adequate. For much of its postwar history, Buick had placed what originally were identified as Ventiports on the front fenders. With the introduction of the Northstar V-8 in the Lucerne CXS model, each front fender received four Ventiports. Buick had dropped an available V-8 in its big car line in the mid–1980s.

The last of four GM divisions to adopt the Northstar V-8 was Buick. In 2008, the engine was a option in the Lucerne Super. In a nod to Buick tradition, four "portholes" were added to the front fenders to note the DOHC V-8 under the hood. Pictured is the 2011 model, the last year of its production (GM Media).

No modification was made to the Northstar V-8 for the Lucerne, and none was needed. The Lucerne was built on the same front-wheel-drive platform and in the same Hamtramck, Michigan, plant as the Cadillac DTS. This Buick, however, was five inches shorter in overall length than the DTS. The Lucerne shared the same Magnetic Ride Control and StabiliTrak system with the Cadillac DTS.

Car & Driver conducted a road test of the 2006 Lucerne CXS for its March issue. Editor Patrick Bedard had more to say about the history of the Ventiports in Buicks over the years than he did about the availability and performance of the Northstar V-8. The addition of the Northstar V-8 in the big Buick was significant because it marked the return of a V-8 to the Buick line after a ten-year absence. However, Bedard did not find this very significant, because he wrote about practically everything else about the car for many paragraphs. This was because, no doubt, he had driven the Chrysler 300 with its 390 lb.-ft. of torque—100 more than the Northstar's maximum torque. Of the Lucerne CXS V-8 performance in comparison to that of the Chrysler V-8, Bedard wrote, "[T]he Lucerne's V-8 is only mildly energetic."[6]

In 2007, the Lucerne Super was introduced at that year's New York Auto Show. The car had a more powerful Northstar V-8, having 292 horse-

The Northstar V-8 as installed in the Buick Lucerne Super (GM Media).

power, but this was at a higher engine rpm, so it was a moot point. The Lucerne V-8 remained in production from 2006 through the 2011 model year. With the demise of the Northstar V-8 that year, Buick reverted to using GM Powertrain V-6 engines in its largest models.

8

Legacy of the Northstar DOHC Multi-valve Engine

The Chevrolet LT5 V-8 and the Cadillac Northstar V-8 were the first, and for a time, the only 32-valve dual overhead cam V-8 engines offered in GM automobiles. The dream of a multi-valve V-12 successor to the Northstar that could have put Cadillac into the upper ranks among premium automotive brands was dashed due to its expense, a severe and long-lasting recession, and other factors. As a sign of how far conventional engine valvetrain technology has come since the 1990s, the standard pushrod overhead valve LT1 V-8 offered in Corvettes today has over 450 horsepower, albeit having 0.5-liter greater displacement than the 5.7 liter LT5.

Nevertheless, in the V-6 engines the corporation offers today, multi-valve engine design is the standard configuration. In fact, the first four-valve-per-cylinder V-6 offered by GM actually followed one year after the 1990 Corvette LT5 and preceded the Northstar V-8 by two years. This 60-degree V-6 with engine code LQ1 was introduced in 1991. It had a displacement of 3.4 liters and used a cogged belt to drive the camshafts instead of chains. It used multi-port fuel injection and developed just over 200 horsepower at 5200 rpm. Detail improvements in the cylinder head and means of fuel injection eventually raised output to 215 horsepower. Between 1991 and 1997, the LQ1 was offered in the Chevrolet Lumina and Monte Carlo, Oldsmobile Cutlass Supreme and Pontiac Grand Prix.

In 1999, Oldsmobile introduced a new multi-valve V-6 based on the L47 V-8 designed for the Aurora model. This engine, the LX5, was designed to power the smaller Intrigue. The LX5 had a 90-degree cylinder bank like the L47, and the cylinder block and cylinder heads were a completely new 3.4 liter design from the 60-degree multi-valve V-6. It had chain-driven dual overhead cams. Curiously, it developed the same horsepower as did the LQ1—215 horsepower. The LX5 came standard in the Oldsmobile Intrigue from 1999 to 2002 and was offered in the Aurora in 2001 and 2002.

The High Feature Naturally Aspirated V-6 Engine Family

General Motors wanted to offer a chain-driven DOHC multi-valve 60-degree V-6 designed from a clean sheet of paper. It would employ new methods of aluminum casting for all the major components, and feature the latest technology in valvetrain design as well as induction. This engine would not only power North American vehicles but be used in GM vehicles manufactured around the world. At the time this engine was conceived, the Chevrolet LT5 had ceased production at the MerCruiser plant in Stillwater, Oklahoma; the Cadillac Northstar V-8 was undergoing refinement of its FWD design and was being redesigned for RWD applications in new Cadillac vehicles. This V-6 engine was a joint design effort

The High Feature V-6 was designed to power an array of GM vehicles beyond Cadillac models, such as this SRX (GM Media).

between Cadillac and GM's Holden division based in Australia. This new V-6 would be offered in displacements from 2.8 to 3.6 liters, but was capable of even greater displacement.

The HFV-6, as it was sometime referred to, was first offered in the 2005 Cadillac CTS in the fall of 2004. The standard V-6 had a displacement of 2.8 liters, having an 89.0 mm bore and a 75 mm stroke. The compression ratio was 10.0:1, requiring premium fuel to supply the sequential multi-port fuel injection system. It developed 210 horsepower at 6500 rpm. Available as an option was the 3.6 liter V-6 having greater bore and stroke with 10.2:1 compression ratio. In the Cadillac CTS this engine, with engine code LY7, was rated at 255 horsepower at 6000 rpm. This 3.6 liter V-6 was also offered in the Cadillac SRX crossover in its first year. In 2005, it also became available in the Buick LaCrosse CXS and Cadillac STS and various Holden models. The LY7 was eventually offered in select Pontiacs, Chevrolets, and Saturns, the GMC Acadia SUV, and even the Suzuki XL7.

In 2006, GM announced the LLT V-6, and this may have been a warning shot to the Northstar V-8 that came standard in the full-size DTS sedan. The LLT V-6 offered direct injection instead of multi-port injection. It also had an impressively high compression ratio of 11.3: 1. This engine produced 302 horsepower at 6300 rpm and 272 lb.-ft. of torque at 5200 rpm. The multi-valve DOHC LLT V-6 had significantly more horsepower than the Northstar V-8, and being a V-6, it also provided better combined fuel economy. This V-6 was not immediately available, however.

The LLT was introduced in the 2008 Cadillac CTS and STS. It was then offered in the Buick Enclave and Chevrolet Traverse SUVs the following year. It subsequently appeared in the 2010 Buick LaCrosse CXS in detuned form having 280 horsepower. For the 2010 Camaro, however, the LLT received some special improvements, both internally and on the exhaust side, to boost horsepower to 312 at 6400 rpm with 278 lb.-ft. of torque at 5200 rpm.

GM Powertrain continued its refinement and improvement of its High Feature V-6, by building on the progress it had originally had made with the LLT. The cylinder head was redesigned, having larger intake valves and longer duration intake camshafts, and now featured an integrated exhaust manifold. This, along with a composite intake manifold, provided a combined weight savings of over 20 pounds for the engine, having the engine code LFX. Horsepower was improved slightly and varied depending on the make and model of vehicle it powered. The LFX first

The High Feature 3.6 liter V-6 engine designed and produced by GM Powertrain features dual overhead camshafts and four valves per cylinder like the Northstar V-8 it replaced, and provided greater performance and gas economy as well (GM Media).

appeared in the 2012 Cadillac SRX crossover and CTS, Chevrolet Camaro and Impala, and Buick LaCrosse. The Camaro received the highest horsepower rating for the LFX, with 323 horsepower at 6800 rpm and 278 lb.-ft. of torque at 4800 rpm as a result of some performance enhancements unique to the Camaro. The LFX remained in production and was offered in various GM vehicles for the next several years.

GM V-6 engine technology is constantly evolving as a part of ongoing product improvement. To improve the naturally aspirated V-6 DOHC design even more, GM Powertrain started with new computer models for practically every part. This engine, with the LGX engine code, has a stiffer and stronger engine block, having a 95mm cylinder bore, and features cast iron bore liners as in previous engines. It features a forged steel crankshaft. The cylinder head was a completely new design having improved, higher-flowing ports. The four-cam phasing system features intermediate park technology that improves fuel efficiency. Even the camshaft timing chain system was redesigned for quieter operation.

The Twin-Turbo LF3

Cadillac had ruled out turbocharging the Northstar V-8 in favor of supercharging for use in V-series of the STS and the XLR. Turbocharging, while a historically proven method of significantly boosting horsepower and torque, had a significant drawback known as "turbo lag." However, GM Powertrain engineers revisited the use of turbocharging on its latest generation V-6 engine. Specifically, ways were investigated to shorten the turbocharging passages, increase the response of the turbochargers, and other means as a way of all but eliminating the annoying turbo lag. These research and development efforts succeeded, and the green light was given to production development of a twin-turbocharged 3.6 liter V-6 engine program.

The product of that program was engine code LF3. Despite the identical displacement and multi-valve DOHC design, most parts of the LF3 engine were a new design. Extensive computer modeling was performed to map the flow of air and air/fuel through the engine in order to make the turbocharging routing as short as possible. Also, with the use of two smaller turbochargers instead of a single, larger turbocharger, response was increased and lag virtually eliminated.

The engine block featured cast-in provisions for turbocharger cooling and lubrication. A forged steel crankshaft was mandatory for this higher output engine. The 10.2:1 compression cylinder heads featured 38.3-mm diameter intake valves and 30.6-mm exhaust valves. These heads incorporated integrated exhaust manifolds. The turbochargers are capable of providing 12 pounds of boost. Cadillac made plans to make available the LF3 in the 2014 CTS sedan as the CTS-V and in the XTS as the XTS

The Twin-Turbo 3.6 liter V-6 produces over 400 horsepower and impressive highway mileage. It is a premium engine option in several Cadillac models and other GM automobiles (GM Media).

VSport. In the CTS-V, the engine was rated at 420 hp at 5750 rpm and 430 lb.-ft. of torque between 3500 and 4500 rpm. The CTS-V achieved a 0–60 mph time of 4.6 seconds and a top speed of 170 mph. In the XTS VSport, the LF3 had 10 less horsepower and significantly less torque.

While online and print magazine editors praised the CTS-V in virtually all areas, especially its straight-line performance and handling, the XTS VSport was not as well-received. Some editors were downright critical of the XTS VSport. Andrew Stoy of *AutoWeek* made it clear he was dis-

The XTS VSport is powered by the twin-turbo LF3 V-6. The engine has received mixed reviews in this Cadillac model (GM Media).

appointed. He wrote: "I'm no fan of Cadillac's 3.6-liter 'high feature' V-6 in any application and it goes about its business in the XTS with its usual lack of refinement. 'But it's the turbo version,' you say, '410 hp!' Tell you what: if you find them, let me know because there was no indication they were under the hood or available at the wheels. Acceleration was unremarkable from both a standing start and during passing. I actually opened the hood when I got home to make sure the turbo engine was in fact installed in our particular car."[1]

Sadly, the other two editors at the magazine, Wes Raynal and Natalie Neff, were similarly unimpressed with the twin-turbo XTS. Neff stated: "There's simply nothing V or sporty about it in the least."

The editors at *Motor Trend* were more charitable (or forgiving). They managed to get the XTS VSport to 60 mph in 5.3 seconds, but other than that, they did not have much else to say about this car's performance. However, the editors at both magazines had praise for the XTS's interior design, appointments and aura of quality.

When the Northstar V-8s, both naturally aspirated and supercharged, were the engines powering Cadillacs, editors were practically unanimous in extolling the virtues of the supremely smooth Northstar V-8 with its impressive power. With the limitations of turbocharging a V-6 engine and installing it in a car weighing over 4000 pounds, the need for a V-8 may once again become of importance to Cadillac.

Another issue is the fact that Cadillac no longer engineers and builds the engines that go into its line of cars. The engines are engineered and built by GM Powertrain. Those engines are designed to go into a range of vehicles, from small two-door coupes to large sedans and even trucks. While Cadillac can engineer its cars and SUVs, the luxury division must take what engines GM Powertrain provides. The engine qualities that drove the design of the Northstar V-8 for Cadillac have been compromised by the General Motors corporate structure.

Some prospective Cadillac owners find it incongruous to have a V-6 engine in a Cadillac. Decades of Cadillac division culture vanished when GM underwent corporate restructuring as a result of the Chapter 11 bankruptcy filing in 2009. The XV12 engine program was canceled and the days of the Northstar V-8 were numbered. The future for Cadillac would be much leaner, while at the same time trying to revitalize its product line and compete with the best that Jaguar, Mercedes-Benz and BMW could deliver.

A New V-8 for Future Cadillacs

In April 2015, Sam Abuelsamid of Navigant Research wrote an article articulating how the V-8s were responsible for the market success of the Cadillac CTS-V and Escalade, but the era of the V-8 in Cadillac large sedans had ended. When he posted the article on Facebook, the new head of Cadillac, Johan De Nysschen, had a sharp rebuttal.

"There absolutely will be another state-of-the-art mega powerful highly efficient new 8-cylinder from Cadillac, besides the CTS-V engine. Purpose-designed for Cadillac. Now, if you consider 'mainstream' to represent the average powertrain used, well, no, the realities of the market today excludes that. Besides the exotics, I don't know that any luxury manufacturer today could claim they sell most of their volume in V-8. But the V-8 Cadillac is alive and well today, and will be in even better shape tomorrow."[2]

De Nysschen's use of the phrase "state-of-the-art" would seem to preclude decades-old pushrod valve-actuation. This is supported by the respected online publication, *GM Authority*. Following the posting of the Navigant Research article, Drew Singer wrote for *GM Authority*: "Nobody is giving exact details, but it's likely the bespoke engine family for Cadillac is going to stray away from the traditional pushrod, OHV V-8 engines that GM has in everything from a Chevrolet Silverado work truck, to the 2015 Corvette Z06, to the upcoming 2016 Cadillac CTS-V and Escalade. It is expected that such a powertrain will end up in a future model year of the Cadillac CT6 and perhaps whatever ends up slotting above it. We'll stop short of saying the Northstar name is coming back, however."[3]

Based on these statements, and the fact DOHC and four-valves-per-cylinder are the most efficient and effective means of generating power, reducing emissions and improving gas mileage, it seems likely that Cadillac will offer a multi-valve DOHC V-8 before 2020. One can be sure that engine sealing will not be an issue with this new engine.

9

The Collectible Northstar V-8 Cadillacs

With every automotive make, model and year, there are occasional collectible cars, and there are forgettable cars. With Cadillac, it goes without saying that the cars of the 1930s are at the very top of collectible cars, and they are priced up to and beyond six figures. The Cadillacs of the mid- to late 1950s and the 1960s are collectible among those who appreciate Cadillacs, but they are rarely seen on the road, and parts are a particular problem for cars of this vintage. During the 1970s, you could single out specific models that would seem to be collectible, such as the 1967 front-wheel drive Eldorado with its timeless and handsome body style, or the 1976 Eldorado Convertible—the last year of that model's production. What makes a Cadillac collectible may have nothing to do with its rarity and more to do with the collector's simply wanting that particular model for personal reasons.

There are definitely Cadillacs that are not in the least collectible. The Seville of the early 1980s was a handsome car, but it has become the object of customizers with an eye for bling, corrupting the car's clean lines, so this car is not collectible. The Cadillac Cimarron, heavily based on the Chevrolet Cavalier, was a forgettable model. The Cadillac Fleetwoods of the late 1980s and early 1990s retained the tailfin design elements which helped define the brand, and in fact the cars remain handsome to this day. The Fleetwood underwent a very successful redesign for 1993 and the new look gave Cadillac an even more elegant and luxurious look. However, it was not powered by the Northstar V-8, but by the LT1 small-block V-8, which also powered the Buick Roadmaster.

Among the Northstar V-8 Cadillacs, the same can also be true. As with every collectible car, the selection can be very subjective. This chapter will be devoted to what makes a certain year and model of Cadillac powered by the Northstar V-8 collectible and what might make it less so. Paramount among the considerations are the Northstar V-8's maintenance and longevity and what the collector should look out for. Not being careful regarding this can cost the buyer thousands in repair bills.

The Northstar V-8 and the Matter of Oil

Precisely because the subject of what makes a car desirable is so subjective and the desire to buy can sometimes be overwhelming because "that beauty might just get away," it pays to look at the Northstar V-8's history of reliability, recalls and maintenance issues before going shopping. It serves as a good reality check that is needed so the buyer does not acquire a repair headache. Although engineered with refinement and surprising power for its displacement, the engine became known as an oil leaker after 80,000 to 100,000 miles. The principal leaks came from the valve covers, cylinder head gasket area, and rear main seal of the engine. This has been true of many automotive engines, but conventional V-8 could often go for many more miles than the Northstar V-8 before oil leaks became a problem. Also, with conventional V-8s, the cost of re-gasketing and resealing the engine was far lower than on a Northstar V-8.

The most reliable source of information on this is from Northstar V-8 mechanics who are familiar with the peculiarities of this engine with regard to oil leaks. In order of mileage-before-replacement, they are:

- The split block seals (between the engine block and lower crankcase at the crankcase centerline) can start leaking as soon as 80,000 miles, and as they deteriorate, the oil leaking will increase. The rear main seal will also deteriorate and contribute to oil leaking between 80,000 and 100,000 miles. To pull the engine and replace these seals can cost upwards of $3000 at a dealer. Naturally, the car should be placed on a lift and the engine should be carefully inspected.
- Cylinder head gaskets and valve cover gaskets can also begin to fail during the above stated mileage figures. These should also be replaced if the main engine seals are being replaced. Northstar V-8 specialist mechanics state that if the Cadillac you are inspecting has over 125,000 miles, you should walk away. At that point, the buyer would soon be facing a complete engine resealing and gasketing if the engine isn't already leaking oil.

• Potential buyers should inspect the radiator expansion tank for engine sealant with the obvious copper particles or dark brown color used in "goop" type engine and radiator sealants. If this is detected, walk away from the purchase.

• In model year 2000, GM Powertrain changed the lower crankcase of the Northstar V-8 from a die-cast part to a high-pressure "squeeze" casting technique to reduce the part's porosity and eliminate oil leaking through the part itself, which was reported on a number of engines.

• In order to avoid the relatively high cost of resealing the high-mileage Northstar V-8 engine, mechanics are recommending simply looking for a lower-mileage Cadillac with 60k to 80k miles or even less. If the car is not a daily driver, the new owner can enjoy his Northstar Cadillac for years before confronting these maintenance repairs.

Other Northstar V-8 Maintenance Issues

Some prospective Cadillac Northstar V-8 car buyers might consider installing a rebuilt engine to replace it, but they will be in for a shock. GM never established a remanufacturing method for the Northstar. There are a number of reasons for this. The engine is very complex due to its DOHC design and other inherent features. Engine remanufacturers have avoided the Northstar V-8 because, for example, the cast-in-place iron liners cannot be overbored—a typical engine remanufacturing step. Certain vital engine parts, like the oversize crankshaft bearings, are unavailable. With respect to worn valve guides, the Cadillac recommendation was to replace the entire cylinder head! Short of complete rebuild, however, there are parts that are recommended to be replaced. The Engine Rebuilders Association recommends replacement of the plastic intake manifold because the complex shape of the manifold may have debris that has collected over the years from various sources, and if the repaired engine has the manifold reinstalled, the debris may have moved inside the manifold and could be ingested during engine startup and may result in damage.

For many OHC engines, valve timing has been controlled by a timing belt, and this would be a routine replacement during a major engine repair or rebuild. The Northstar V-8 employed timing chains and these typically do not require replacement.

During the production lifetime of the Northstar V-8, GM Powertrain continually made improvements to the engine, too numerous to list here.

As issues with the engine were encountered by owners and repair issues were filtered up to GM, service bulletins were issued on how to resolve the problem, and that in turn was passed on to manufacturing so upgrades to the engine could be implemented. Generally speaking, Northstar V-8s from the 2000s should be less problematic than the earlier engines built in the 1990s. However, the ultimate determining factor, as it has been for all automotive engines, is mileage.

Another key thing to consider in the purchase of a Northstar V-8–powered Cadillac is the transmission. Naturally, if any delayed shifting is detected during test driving, this is one Cadillac you should walk away from, unless you are prepared to have a transmission overhaul performed. Inspect the transmission fluid for signs of burnt fluid and discoloration. Always ask to see the vehicle maintenance records. If none are available for the car, that should be a red flag.

The Northstar V-8 was actually part of the Northstar System when first introduced. This included advanced suspension control and braking systems. Over the years, Cadillac improved and added to the vehicle's suspension sophistication to offer the optimum in ride and handling. The earliest generation of this was the Road Sensing Suspension (RSS), which was refined over the years to the latest Continuously Variable Road Sensing Suspension (CVRSS) 2.0. This system senses road conditions, vehicle speed and handling inputs to optimize damping and firmness at each wheel in real time. In addition, Cadillac developed StabiliTrak to help maintain vehicle stability. Finally, some Cadillacs were available with Magnetic Ride Control. When considering the purchase of a Northstar Cadillac, be sure to find out the condition of these suspension and braking systems as well. You may find parts in these systems are worn and need to be replaced.

Smart car buyers should always pay for a vehicle background check like that available from Carfax. The reasonable cost is well worth it to get a complete repair, recall and accident history of the vehicle. And always ask to have your mechanic inspect it bumper to bumper. An owner who has maintained his car well will have no problem with this request.

The Cadillac of Your Dreams

There are some universal qualities of Cadillacs of the Northstar era that make ownership a real pleasure. Beginning with the engine, Cadillac and then GM Powertrain designed and refined it to offer unprecedented refinement, smoothness, fuel economy and performance. It was indeed a premium V-8, as the corporation viewed the engine. Supercharged versions of the Northstar were among the most powerful yet refined powerplants in the world. The level of ownership satisfaction with the Northstar V-8 underhood was always high.

Apart from the powertrain, Cadillac style was also at the top of the buyer's list of desirable qualities. There were some stunning-looking Cadillacs during the 1990s and early 2000s, as well as some not-so-good-looking models. Beauty has always been in the eye of the beholder, but this book will point out some of the better-looking models that help to give the car a timeless look.

Finally, there is the interior. Whether the car was a Seville, Eldorado, DeVille or other model, the sumptuous leather seating was among the most handsome and comfortable in the world. The most worn seating of the vehicle would of course be the driver's seat, but oftentimes you will find the remaining seating looks virtually new, especially if the car or SUV was garage-stored. The leather provides a cool, breathable seating surface, and just the right amount of grip to prevent sliding. In addition, there may be some electronic systems or readouts in the instrument cluster that need replacing. Try to determine what the cost would be to replace them.

Below are individual listings for the most desirable of the Northstar Cadillacs, and those with automotive significance of interest to collectors. Remember, these models may not increase in value as a collectible car, but they are collectible to the owner who wants to enjoy driving it.

The 1993 Allanté

The two-seater roadster with body designed and built by Pininfarina of Italy was introduced for the 1987 model year. The original showcar by Pininfarina was considerably more stylish; the production car was more conservatively styled. It was introduced with Cadillac's 4.1 liter engine rated at 170 horsepower. This engine remained the only powerplant in the Allanté until the last model year of 1993. That year Cadillac rolled out the Northstar V-8 in the Allanté. The DOHC 275 horsepower Northstar V-8 transformed the car, and by then, numerous other issues had been resolved to make this the best year of the Allanté's production run. However, the list price for the car had by that point risen to over $60,000. This was the

The Allanté body was designed by Pininfarina of Italy. The Northstar V-8 was only available in 1993—the last year of the car's production (GM Media).

most expensive postwar production Cadillac. Nevertheless, lovers of the Allanté have often owned several of them, and that may be the real meaning of "collectible."

The Seville SLS and STS (1993–2004)

In 1992 Cadillac rolled out the completely redesigned Seville. The new design of the Seville was completely its own, as opposed to the previous generation, which shared the body with other GM divisions. The formal notchback roofline of the outgoing model gave it a generic look that made it difficult to distinguish from a Buick or Oldsmobile from the rear. The sleek new Seville SLS (Seville Luxury Sedan) was a stunning styling statement that was handsome from every angle. Riding on a spacious 111-inch wheelbase, the four-door sedan offered plenty of leg room for rear passengers. Outward visibility was excellent thanks to the Seville's thoughtful design. The optional leather seating surfaces were what buyers had come to expect from Cadillac, and luxurious ebony wood trim pieces added to the interior's elegance. The standard engine in 1992 was the 4.9 liter OHV V-8. The Seville STS (Seville Touring Sedan) sported monochromatic (color matching) grille, quicker steering, console mounted gear selector, and beefier stabilizer bars. The STS came standard with the leather seating surfaces. By and large, the Seville SLS and STS received high marks from *Consumer Guide* and automotive publications for the car's looks, as well as its improved ride and handling.

In 1994, the Northstar V-8 became the standard powerplant in the Seville, and it was available in two states of tune. The SLS came with the 275-hp Northstar, and the STS was powered by the 295-hp version having a revised cam profile. The SLS came with Speed Sensitive Suspension, while the STS was equipped with Road Sensing Suspension and traction control. This remained the Seville's offerings with minor changes in paint color and options. In 1998 the Seville underwent a subtle softening of its lines done more for the sake of change than any improvement in the car's looks. It kept this look through the end of its production run of 2004. The last production year for the STS was 2003 and for the SLS, 2004.

It should be noted the FWD Seville did not benefit from the engineering and performance enhancements incorporated in the RWD Northstar V-8. It did eventually receive a forged steel crankshaft, but the engine did not receive VVT. Nevertheless, this last generation of the Seville was

Among the best-looking Northstar-powered Cadillacs are the Seville SLS and STS from 1994 to 1997. The highest production year was 1994 with over 46,700 units built (GM Media).

The Seville was modestly redesigned for 1998, but this did not help boost sales, which continued to decline. The last production year for the Seville was 2004 (GM Media).

absolutely the best, and if you can find a low-mileage model it would prove most enjoyable to own and drive.

Eldorado and ETC (1992–2003)

The two-door Eldorado had been Cadillac's flashiest model since 1952. The car went through a much-needed downsizing during the 1980s. But then the pendulum swung the other way, and in 1992 the Eldorado was introduced with a completely unique look shared with no other GM car. This last generation rode on a 108-inch wheelbase and had a longer overall length (compared to 1991) of 202 inches. The lines on this Eldorado were crisp and angular, and shared no sheet metal with the Buick Riviera riding on the same platform.

In 1993, the Eldorado was again powered by the OHV 4.9 liter Cadillac V-8, but the sport version, the ETC (Eldorado Touring Coupe) was powered by the 4.6 liter Northstar V-8 rated at 295 hp, the same engine offered in the Seville STS. The 1994 Eldorado did get the 275 hp Northstar V-8. The Eldorado underwent a subtle change in bumper design in 1995

The two-door Eldorado coupe featured more sharply defined body lines than the Seville. Shown is the Eldorado European Touring Coupe (ETC) from 2000 (GM Media).

that imperceptibly shortened the car. It retained the same edgy body design for the remainder of its production run through 2002. What makes this generation of Eldorado particularly collectible are the timeless body design and the engine under the hood. This Eldorado's body is so perfectly realized, it remains handsome and undated. This cannot be said of the previous generation Eldorado.

The level of satisfaction among current Eldorado owners is high, for the above stated reasons. More than a few owners related in reviews of this car that their Eldorado often gets admiring looks from passersby, and this for a car design that is over 20 years old. That is what makes this car a particularly good choice when looking for a Northstar V-8–powered Cadillac.

Sedan DeVille and Concours (1994–1999)

The largest sedan powered by the Northstar V-8 was the Sedan DeVille. The iconic model was successfully redesigned for 1994 with a clean new front-end design and full flanks and hint of fins at the rear. The DeVille rode on a 113.8-inch wheelbase and had an overall length of nearly 210 inches. While the 1994 DeVille came powered by the OHV 4.9 liter V-8, Cadillac introduced a new model that year called the Concours (the "s" is silent), powered by the 270 hp Northstar LD8 V-8 having a cam profile better suited for torque to move the heavy sedan at lower rpms. In 1996 the DeVille finally received the Northstar V-8 and the Concours received a higher-rated L37 Northstar V-8 with 300 hp. Thus, the 1996 Cadillac Concours was the most powerful full-size Cadillac sedan and would be worth owning provided the mileage was reasonable.

For 1998, the DeVille received a redesigned front end that successfully updated the look of the car while retaining an unmistakable Cadillac look. This front-end design was retained through the 1999 model year. However, the DeVille was about to undergo a complete redesign. The 2000 model was all new from bumper to bumper and rode on a longer 115.3-inch wheelbase. Reviews of the car's appearance were mixed. The design of the odd-looking headlights and nondescript grille came in for criticism. However, Cadillac had also done considerable work on the chassis structure and suspension. *Car & Driver*'s editors were impressed with the handling capabilities of the DeVille DTS—the model that replaced the Concours.

The DeVille from 1994 remains a handsome full-size sedan to this day. Most examples you find will have high mileage, but there just may be a "barn find" with less than 60,000 miles that would make this a worthwhile collectible (GM Media).

The DeVille retained this sheet metal through the 2005 model year. The FWD Northstar V-8 during this time did receive a forged steel crankshaft which was also used in the RWD Northstar V-8s. However, the FWD Northstars did not receive the Variable valve timing, which was employed only on the RWD engine.

The DTS (2006–2011)

As the saying goes, all things come to those who wait. In 2006, Cadillac replaced the DeVille with the DTS and an entirely new body design yet again. The DTS rode on a 115.6-inch wheelbase and the body design employed the Art & Science philosophy going throughout the entire Cadillac line. One has to admit the redesign of Cadillac's full-size sedan was successful. The two engines offered in the DTS were the 275 horsepower LD8 or the 291–292 horsepower L37. Horsepower varied slightly on the L37 depending on the model year and the fact the rating was taken at two different rpms.

What makes this last generation full-size Cadillac design the most collectible of all was the latest design for the rigid body structure providing

The DTS (for DeVille Touring Sedan) was the last full-size sedan to be powered by the Northstar V-8. Its last production year was 2011. Many are still on the road today (GM Media).

the best possible handling, the Northstar V-8 having all the latest improvements and performance enhancements, and the DTS body design that will age very gracefully, if at all. There is another DTS model that should not be overlooked for collectibility. That is the DTS-L. This was a modestly stretched DTS built by Accubuilt, having an 8.0-inch longer wheelbase to provide even more leg room for rear passengers. The car retained the good lines of the DTS without taking on the bizarre look of the much longer stretch limousines. The DTS-L is a rare vehicle, and by its nature would have very low miles. However, the custom nature of the DTS-L and very limited production will make this an expensive car to consider.

When Cadillac announced the end of the Northstar V-8 production for 2010, the division later extended the production year of the DTS through 2011, so that was the last production year of this model. The DTS will remain an excellent choice for prospective buyers of a Northstar V-8–powered Cadillac. This is especially true since the replacement for the DTS, the XTS introduced for 2012, came standard with a V-6 engine with no V-8 option available.

The STS and STS-V (2005–2011)

To replace the Seville SLS and STS, Cadillac introduced the new generation RWD STS for 2005. It rode on a 116.4-inch wheelbase and came standard with a V-6, but it was the 320 horsepower LH2 Northstar V-8 that made the new sedan interesting. The engine got the additional horsepower through various engine improvements, including the variable valve timing (VVT). When the STS was engineered, Cadillac wanted all-wheel drive (AWD) to also be available as an option.

For 2006, Cadillac offered the high-performance STS-V model with the 4.4 liter Northstar SC V-8 with an impressive 469 horsepower with an equally impressive 439 lb.-ft. of torque. It had a base list price just over $77,000. The supercharged Northstar V-8 raised Cadillac performance to a whole new level unavailable in the FWD cars. Cadillac boldly stated a 0–60 mph time of under five seconds right in its brochures. It could easily cruise at 140 mph, but its top speed was governor-limited. The STS-V came standard with Brembo brakes. The STS and STS-V were development tested at Germany's Nürburgring race track. The car received very favorable reviews from the mainline magazine editors who tested it. The body

The STS-V was a conservatively styled smaller RWD sedan, but was powered by the supercharged Northstar V-8 and is worth considering as a collectible (GM Media).

received a subtle redesign in 2008. The STS-V was last offered in 2009. The last production year of the STS with the Northstar V-8 was 2010.

The XLR and XLR-V (2004–2009)

In the six production years for the XLR and its high-performance variant the XLR-V, just over 15,000 cars were built at the Bowling Green, Kentucky, plant. The peak production years were 2004, 2005 and 2006. According to General Motors media database, 3,665 were built in 2004, 3,730 in 2005 and 3,203 in 2006. Sales dropped dramatically after that. So the most plentiful supply of XLRs will be found between 2004 and 2006.

The XLR was easily Cadillac's most expensive model. The 2004 XLR had a base list price of $75,435. It was powered by the 320-horsepower RWD Northstar V-8. Examples with reasonable mileage can be found today for roughly one third of its original list price, which makes the XLR an affordable proposition for the Cadillac collector. Subsequent years had incrementally higher prices.

The XLR-V, introduced for 2006, was the fastest production Cadillac ever built up to that time. That acceleration and top speed came with a hefty price, with the 2006 model listing for just under $100,000. The XLR-V could accelerate to 60 mph in under five seconds and had a governor-limited top speed of 155 mph. What also makes the XLR and XLR-V collectible is the car's maintenance history. XLR owners by and large keep meticulous maintenance and repair records, and prospective owners can usually see the entire history of the car. The XLR is certainly one of the most significant Cadillac models built in the company's history and nothing looks like it on the road. Stylistically, it closely approaches the Evoq concept car. It is perhaps the most collectible of Cadillacs powered by the Northstar or Northstar SC V-8.

The SRX V-8 (2004–2009)

The SRX was introduced for 2004 not so much as a sport utility vehicle (SUV) but, as *Car & Driver* identified it, "a tall station wagon." The editor actually thought of the SRX as more of a truck with extra carrying capacity than a car. The SRX rode on a 116.4-inch wheelbase and was one of the heaviest vehicles in the Cadillac line, weighing over 4,400 pounds.

The XLR-V with supercharged Northstar V-8 and head-turning looks ranks as the most collectible Cadillac with the multi-valve DOHC V-8 (GM Media).

The SRX was RWD and the 320-horsepower Northstar V-8 was required to give the vehicle sufficient performance in all situations. It could accelerate to 60 mph in 6.6 seconds and had a top speed of 144 mph.

The looks of the SRX were very much a subjective call. The vehicle was not a beauty, in the opinion of this author, but then this was a utilitarian vehicle. It reflected the Art & Science design philosophy, particularly the front end; the remaining part of the vehicle was boxy in appearance. However, for buyers wanting a Northstar V-8 to haul people and extra stuff, the SRX could very well fit the bill.

In 2004, it had a base list price right around $47,000, and a decade later, these vehicles could be had for around $10,000 to $12,000. Low-mileage versions (under 80,000 miles) would go for more. This would make a very affordable transport for a family and their luggage. The SRX is not really a collectible, but it is luxurious and practical.

In 2010, Cadillac introduced the next-generation SRX and it won kudos for its handsome design. However, the Northstar V-8 was no longer available, and it was only available with a selection of three different V-6 engines.

As noted in the previous chapter on the legacy of the Northstar V-8, today's GM V-6 engines provide significantly better fuel economy, performance and engine sealing over the Northstar V-8. The original Northstar V-8 was the last V-8 engine designed by that GM division's own engineers. It is a milestone engine in the history of Cadillac, and if for no other reason, this makes it collectible.

Chapter Notes

Introduction

1. Maurice D. Hendry and the Editors of Automobile Quarterly, *Cadillac, Standard of the World: The Complete History* (Princeton, 1977), p. 30.

2. Alfred P. Sloan, *My Years with General Motors* (Doubleday, 1963), p. 7. Sloan commented in his autobiography that Buick accounted for most of GM's car production and 20 percent of automobile output in the United States. He wrote the remaining cars built by GM, including Cadillac, "were of little consequence."

3. Hendry, p. 102.

4. Daniel Alef, *The Fabulous Fisher Brothers* (Titans of Fortune, 2007), pp. 2–3.

5. Sloan, pp. 268–269.

6. Mary Sieber and Ken Buttolph, *Standard Catalog of Cadillac 1912–1990* (Iola, WI: Krause, 1991, pp. 148–149.

7. Sieber and Buttolph, p. 201.

8. Hendry, p. 342.

9. Sieber and Buttolph, p. 255.

Chapter 2

1. *The Northstar DOHC V-8 Engine for Cadillac*, James E. Foss, Robert L. Jacques, Richard A. Marsh, and Philip J. Brooks, SAE Technical Paper No. 920671, February 1992.

2. "'98 Cadillac Seville—First Drive," *Motor Trend*, October 1997.

3. "Cadillac DeVille," *Car & Driver*, September 1999.

4. "2006 Cadillac DTS," *Car & Driver*, September 2006.

Chapter 3

1. Michael J. Bonello, James D. Cremonesi, Richard S. Davis, Gregory P. Prior, and John C. Zinser, *The Next Generation Northstar DOHC 4.6L Engine with Four-Cam Continuously Variable Valve Timing for Cadillac*. SAE Document No. 2003–01–0922, 2003.

2. Bonello, et al.

3. Bonello, et al.

4. GM Powertrain press release, "GM Adopts New Manufacturing Strategy at Livonia Engine Plant to Achieve Best-in-Class Northstar Quality," September 5, 2002.

5. GM Powertrain press release, "Next-Generation Northstar Sets New Standard in Performance and Refinement for Cadillac XLR, SRX," September 5, 2002.

6. "Battlestar Cadillac-tica," *Road & Track*, June 2003.

7. *Road & Track*, June 2003.

8. "Cadillac stakes a claim in the luxury-roadster arena," *Car & Driver*, June 2003.

9. "Cadillac SRX V-8," *Car & Driver*, September 2003.

10. *Car & Driver*, September 2003.

11. *Car & Driver*, November 2005.

Chapter 4

1. John McCormick, *Cadillac XLR* (Ann Arbor, MI: World House, 2003).

2. GM Press Release, *GM Unleashes Northstar 4.4-Liter Supercharged V-8 for 2006 Cadillac STS-V and XLR-V*, March 23, 2005.

3. *The Supercharged Northstar DOHC 4.4L V8 Engine for Cadillac*. M. Bonello, D. Caldwell, J. Pigott, P. Prior, and T. Schag. SAE Paper No. 2005–01–1854, SAE International (2005).

4. *Hydra-Matic Transmissions*, GM Powertrain brochure and CD, January 2005.

5. Matt DeLorenzo, "Back in the Game," *Car & Driver*, January 2005.

6. Steve Dulcich, editor, "Cadillac Power—

Blown, Injected, and 1.65 HP per Cube," *Popular Hot Rodding,* January 2009.

7. *Road & Track* web link, May 18, 2006. http://www.roadandtrack.com/car-reviews/road-test-updates/cadillac-xlr-v. Accessed December 15, 2012.

Chapter 5

1. Karl Ludvigsen, *The V12 Engine: The Untold Story of Technology, Evolution, Performance and Impact of All* (Haynes Publishing, 2005).

2. Karl Ludvigsen, *The V12 Engine: The Untold Story of Technology, Evolution, Performance and Impact of All* (Haynes Publishing, 2005).

3. Kevin Jost, "Cien Showcases Northstar XV12," general press release, August 20, 2001.

4. Alex Law, "GM's Northstar XV12 Engine Takes Advance of Several Technological Advances," September 11, 2001. http://www.auto123.com. Accessed October 18, 2009.

5. GM Inside News, "IL Insider: Cadillac Shelves the Twelve," August 21, 2008. http://www.gminsidenews.com/forums/f21/il-insider-cadillac-shelves-twelve-68337/. Accessed March 24, 2012.

6. Keith Naughton, "The Fast and the Luxurious," *Newsweek,* January 12, 2003.

7. Alcoa Press release, "Alcoa and General Motors Combine Design, Engineering Talents to Create Cadillac Sixteen Concept Car, and Ultimate Luxury Sedan," January 6, 2003.

8. *Newsweek*, January 12, 2003.

9. Cadillac Press release, "Cadillac Sixteen's Aluminum Content Beyond Conventional." January 5, 2003.

10. "Katech Caddy—1000hp V-16 Buildup," *Engines,* Summer 2003.

11. Cadillac Press Release, "GM Cadillac Sixteen Concept 2003," January 5, 2003.

12. *Newsweek*, January 12, 2003

13. Cadillac Press release, "The Cadillac Sixteen," January 5, 2003.

14. GM Press Release, "GM's Innovative XV16 Concept Engine Looks to Past and Future," January 5, 2003.

Chapter 6

1. Lawrence W. Berman, "The LeMans Era," Briggs Cunningham American Racing Tradition. http://www.briggscunningham.com. Accessed 03/27/2013.

2. Press Release, "IRL: Aurora V8 has first run on a dyno," GM Motorsports, September 27, 1996. Note: Complete design and development of the IRL Aurora V-8 is covered in SAE Paper No. 983037, R. Allen, N. Baker, E. Keating, et al., "IRL Aurora V8 Design and Development."

3. Press Release, "IRL: Indy 500 Aurora V8 Wins Award," GM Motorsports, May 15, 1997.

4. Press Release, "2000 Cadillac Northstar Le Mans Prototype," Cadillac North America, undated.

5. "2000 Cadillac Northstar Le Mans Prototype," Riley & Scott Technical Description, Indianapolis, Indiana, 1999.

6. Gary S. Vasilash, "Powertrain Performers," *Automotive Design & Production*, December 2000.

7. "Powertrain Performers," *Automotive Design & Production*, January 1, 2001. http://www.autofieldguide.com/articles/powertrain-performers.

8. Racing Sports Cars, LMP Results for 2000. http://www.racingsportscars.com/type/results/Cadillac/Northstar_LMP_2000.

9. GM Racing Press Release, March 28, 2001.

10. Racing Sports Cars, LMP-00-004 and LMP-00-006 Results. http://www.racingsportscars.com/make/results/Cadillac.html?page=2

11. "Cadillac LMP 02 Technical Insights: Chassis Design and Development," *Total MotorSport.*

12. "Cadillac LMP 02 Technical Insights: Northstar Engine Development," GM Racing Communications, January 14, 2002.

13. "Cadillac LMP 02 Technical Insights: Chassis Design and Development," GM Racing Communications, January 14, 2002.

14. Racing Sports Cars, All Results of Cadillac (page 2): http://www.racingsportscars.com/make/results/Cadillac.html?page=2

Chapter 7

1. "Oldsmobile Aerotech," http://www.outrightolds.com/index.php/spotlight-on/olds-aerotech; "Oldsmobile Aerotech," Generations of GM History, GM Heritage Center, https://history.gmheritagecenter.com/wiki/index.php/Oldsmobile_Aerotech.

2. *Motor Trend*, September 1994.
3. "One Year: 1995 Aurora Long Term Wrap Up," *Motor Trend*, June 1996. http://www.motortrend.com/roadtests/oneyear/112_9606_1995_oldsmobile_aurora/viewall.html.
4. "Road Test: 2001 Oldsmobile Aurora 4.0," *Motor Trend*, April 2001.
5. "2004 Chrysler 300 vs. Ford Crown Victoria, Pontiac Bonneville," *Car & Driver*, September 2004.
6. "2006 Buick Lucerne CXS," *Car & Driver*, March 2006.

Chapter 8

1. *AutoWeek*, "2014 Cadillac XTS VSport review notes," December 4, 2013.
2. "Cadillac to Get New, Unique V-8 Despite Talk of the V-8's Death," by Nelson Ireson, *Motor Authority*, April 16, 2015. http://www.motorauthority.com/news/1097854_cadillac-to-get-new-unique-v-8-despite-talk-of-the-v-8s-death.
3. "Johan de Nysschen Has to Remind the Internet That Cadillac Will Get New V8 Engines," by Drew Singer, *GM Authority*, April 17, 2015. http://gmauthority.com/blog/2015/04/johan-de-nysschen-has-to-remind-the-internet-that-cadillac-will-get-new-v8-engines/.

Bibliography

Alef, Daniel. *The Fabulous Fisher Brothers.* N.p.: Meta4press, 2009.

Bonello, Michael, et al. *The Next Generation Northstar 4.6L DOHC V8 with Four-Cam Continuously Variable Valve Timing for Cadillac.* SAE Paper No. 2003–01-0922. Warrendale, PA: SAE International, 2003.

Bonello, Michael, et al. *The Supercharged Northstar DOHC 4.4L V8 Engine.* SAE Paper No. 2005–01-1854. Warrendale, PA: SAE International, 2005.

Buttolph, Ken, and Mary Sieber. *Standard Catalog of Cadillac 1912–1990.* Krause Publications, 1991.

Foss, James E., et al. *The Northstar DOHC V-8 for Cadillac.* SAE Paper No. 1992–02-01. Warrendale, PA: SAE International, 1992.

Hendry, Maurice D. *Cadillac, Standard of the World: The Complete History.* New York: Automobile Quarterly, 1977.

Ludvigsen, Karl. *The V12 Engine: The Untold Story of Technology, Evolution, Performance and Impact of All V12-Engined Cars.* Sparkford: Haynes Publishing, 2005.

McCormick, John. *Cadillac XLR.* Ann Arbor, MI: Word House, 2003.

Young, Anthony. *The Heart of the Beast: History of the LT5 V-8 and ZR-1 Corvette.* New York: Automobile Quarterly, 1999.

Index